SEX

Mania

RAVETTE BOOKS

This edition published by
Ravette Books Limited
© Ravette Books Limited 1994

Printed and bound in Great Britain
for Ravette Books Limited,
25/31 Tavistock Place
London WC1H 9SU
An Egmont Company
by Cox & Wyman Ltd.
Reading

Editor: Nigel Foster
Illustrated by: Charles Hemming

ISBN: 1 85304 403 2

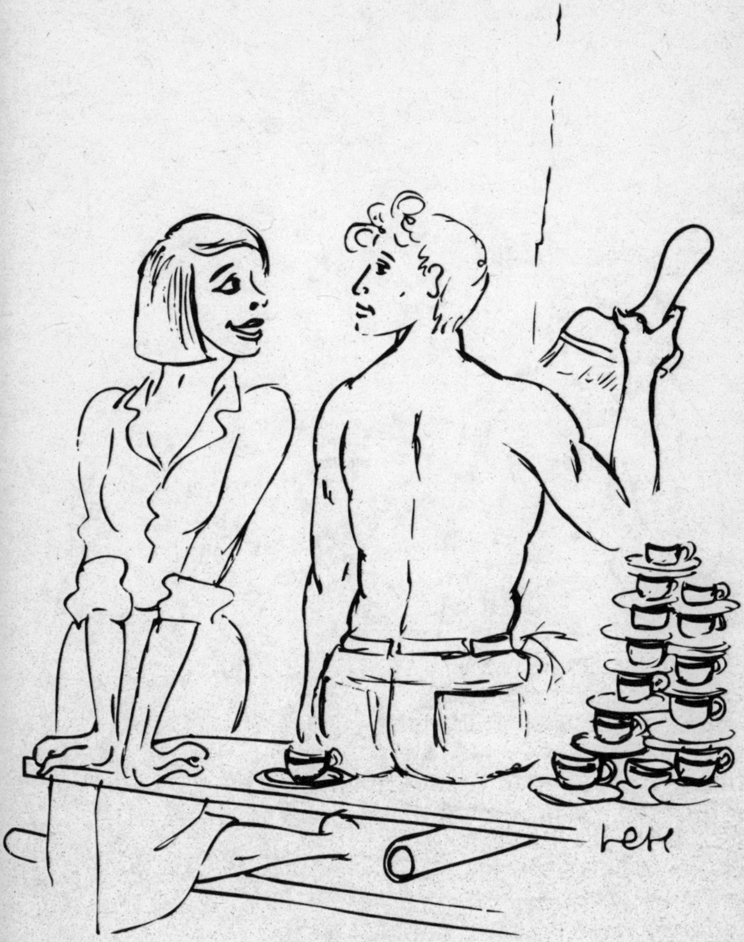
Lee

'How about another cup of coffee?'

'Just like your wife. Cold feet, cold hands . . . cold . . .'

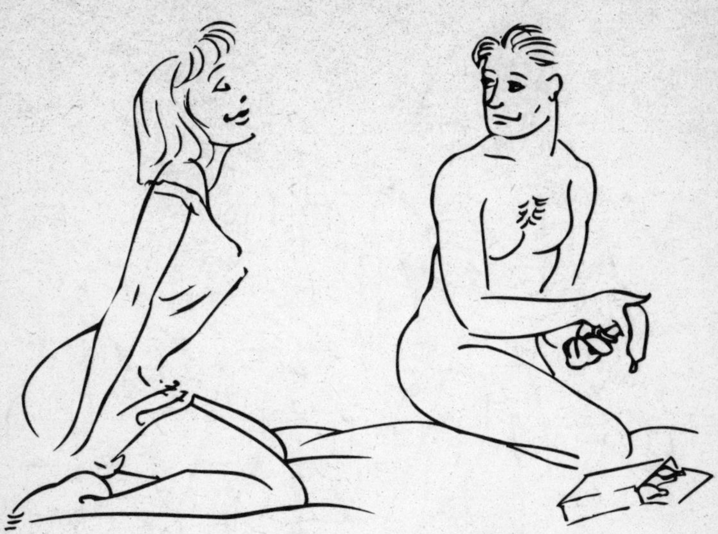

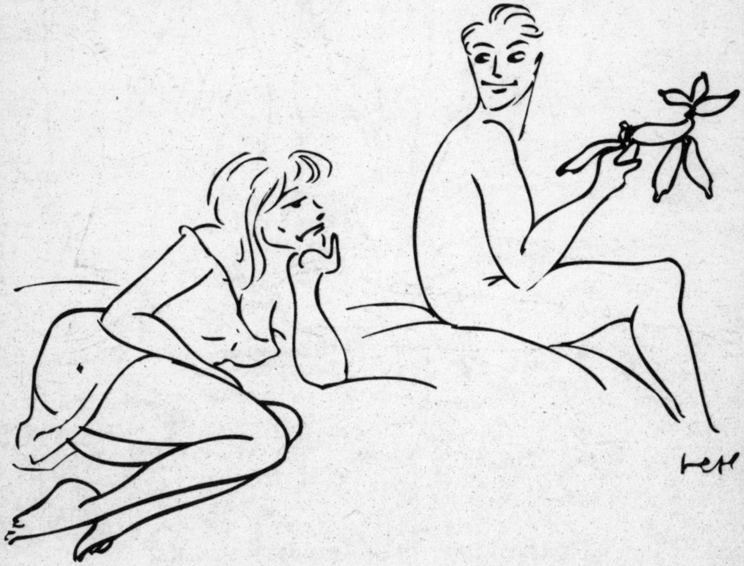

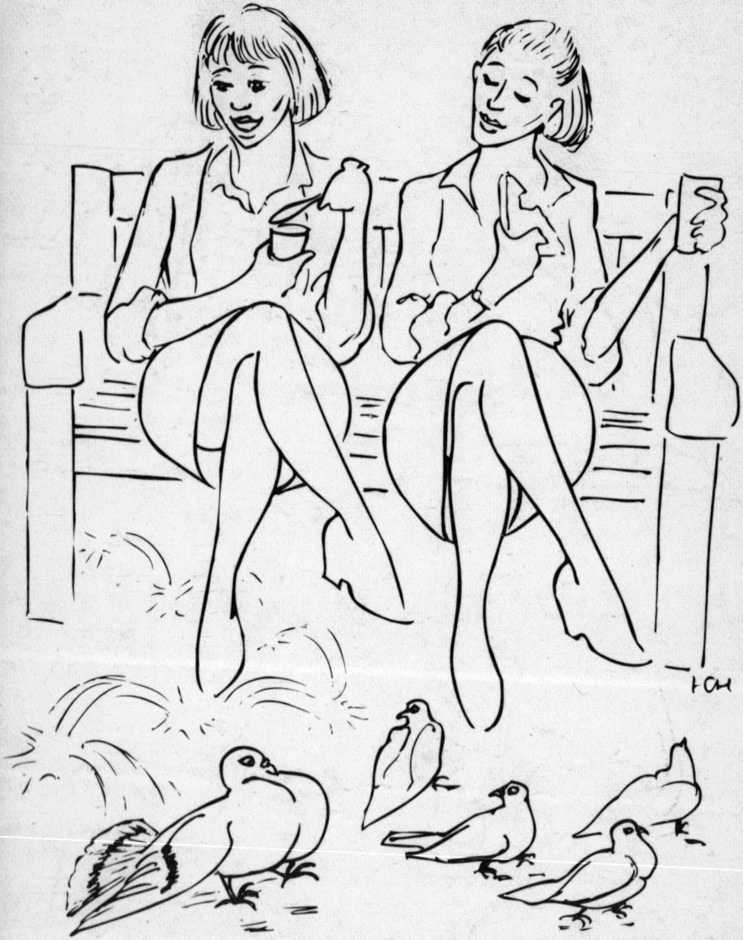

'He reminds me of Ken in Accounts.'

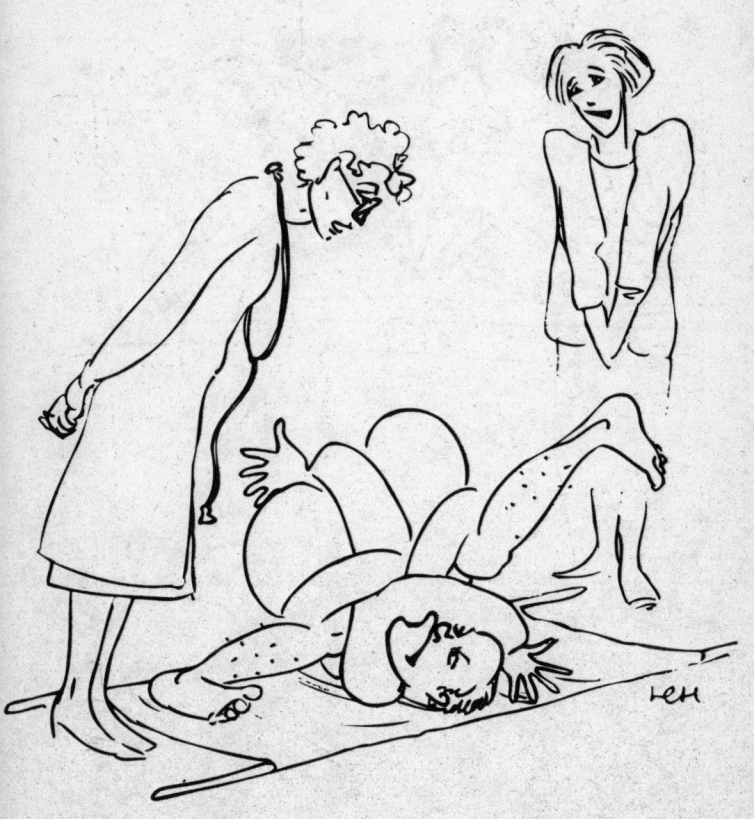

'The idea is that you read "The Art of Love" together, *not* on your own!'

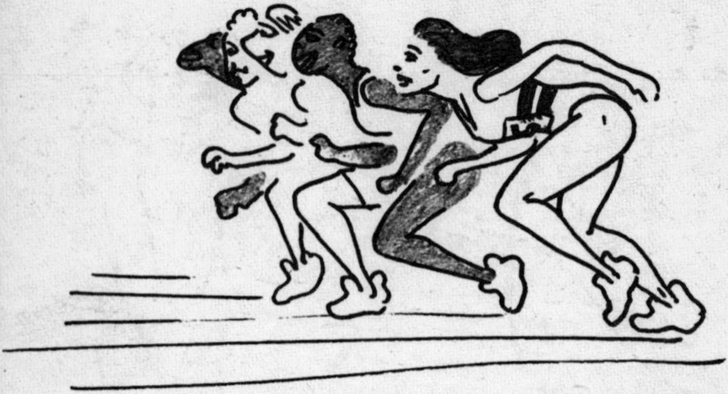

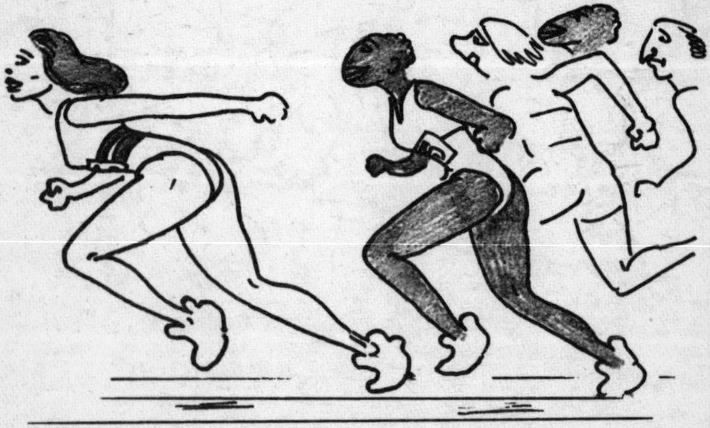

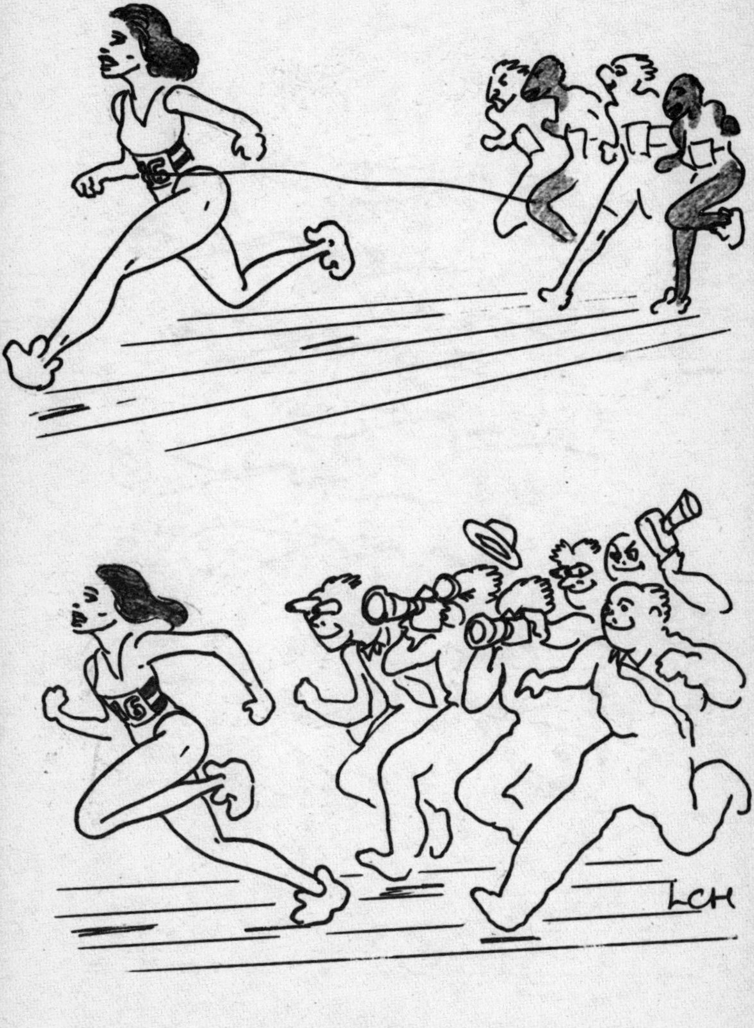
16
16
LCH

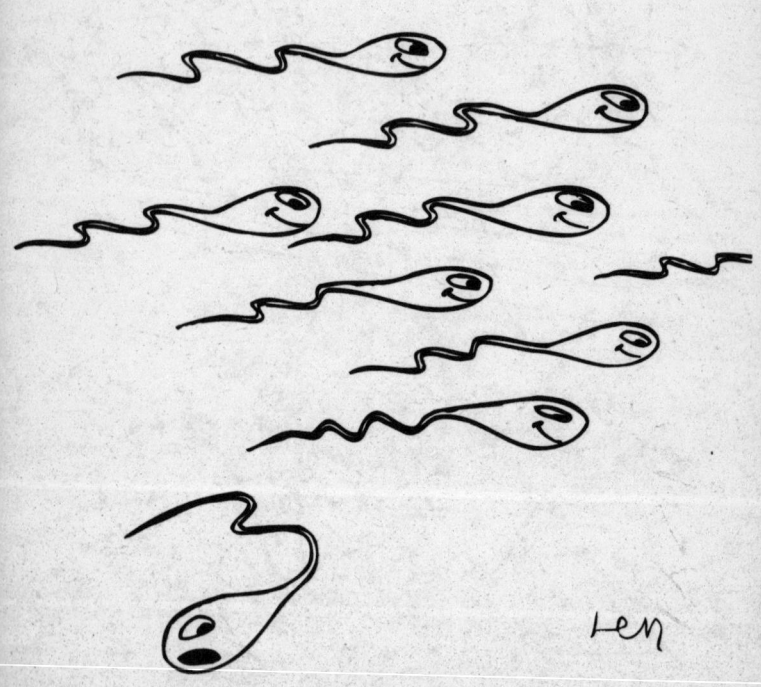

'Okay. So you guys can risk a paternity suit!'

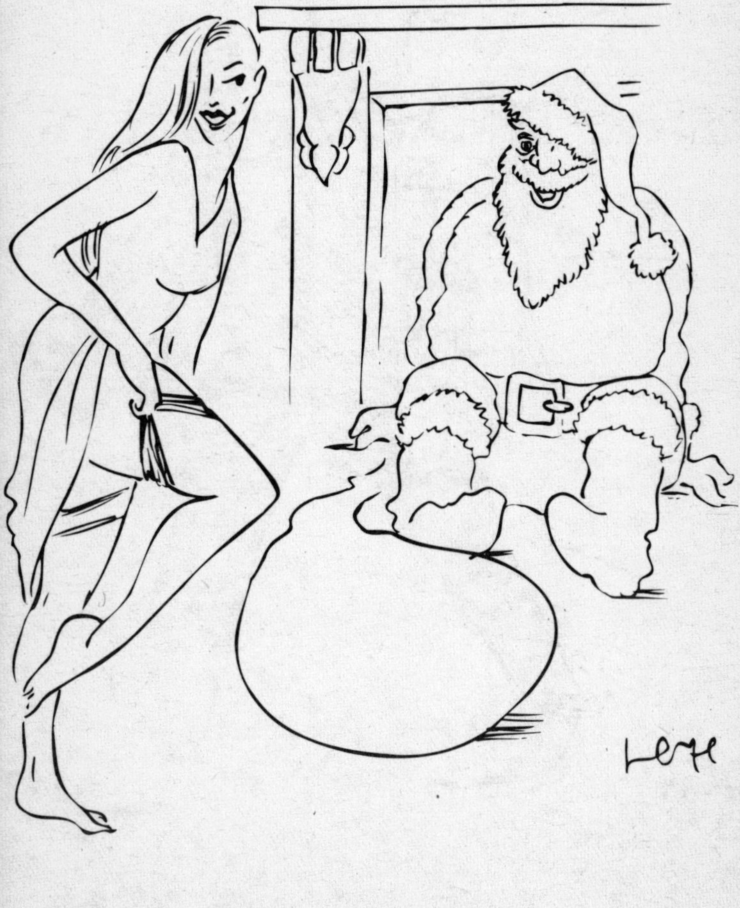

'I thought I'd fill my stocking before you got here . . .'

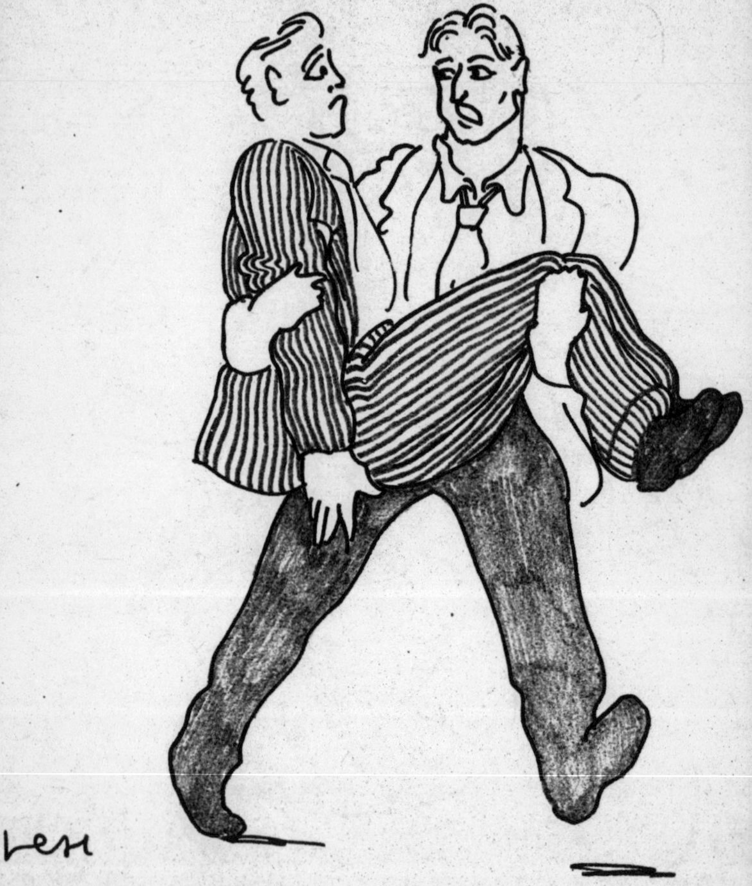

'Sometimes, Miles, a man's gotta do what a man's gotta do . . .'

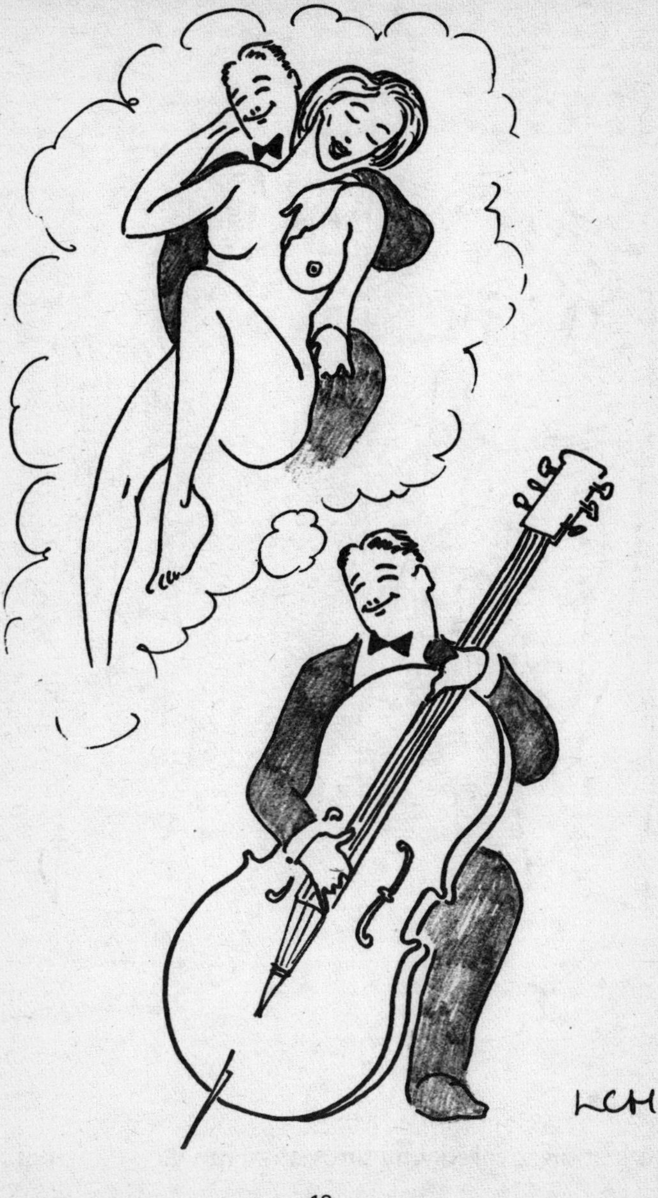

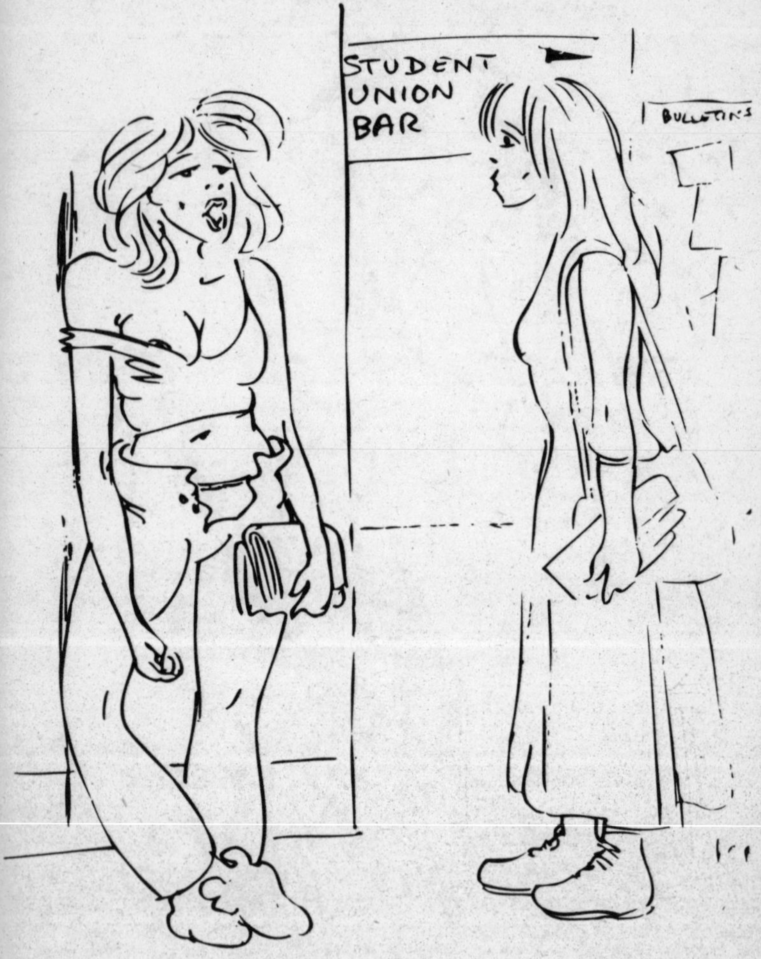
STUDENT
UNION
BAR
BULLETINS
'I've just discovered why he's called the Vice-Principal . . .'

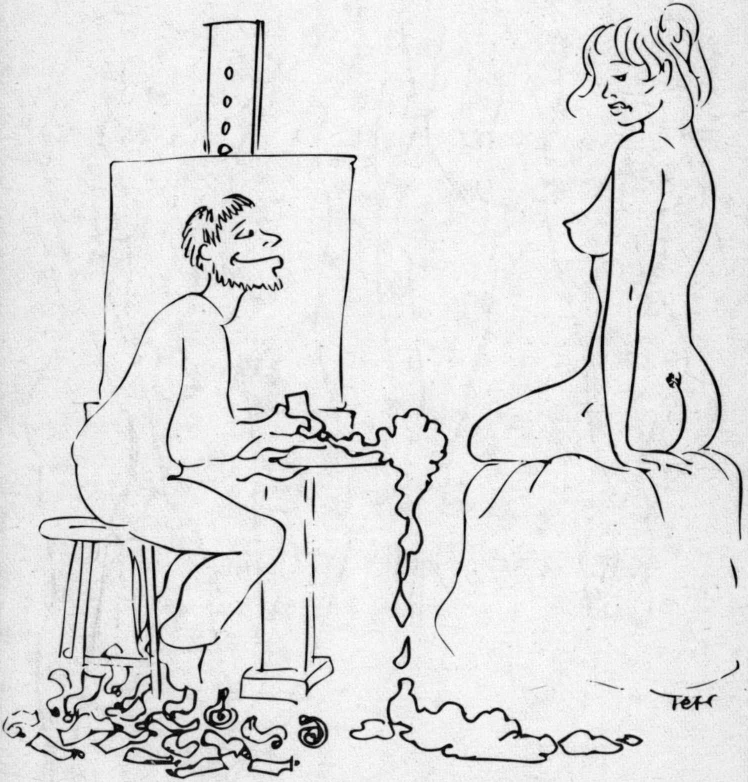

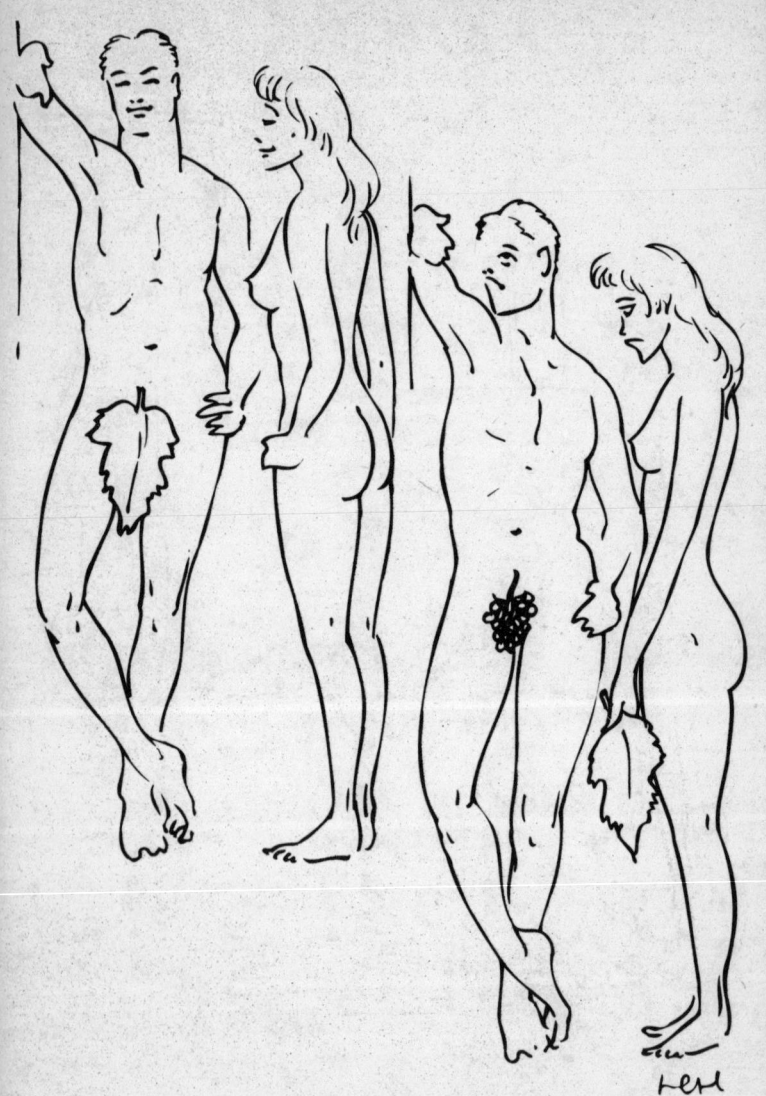

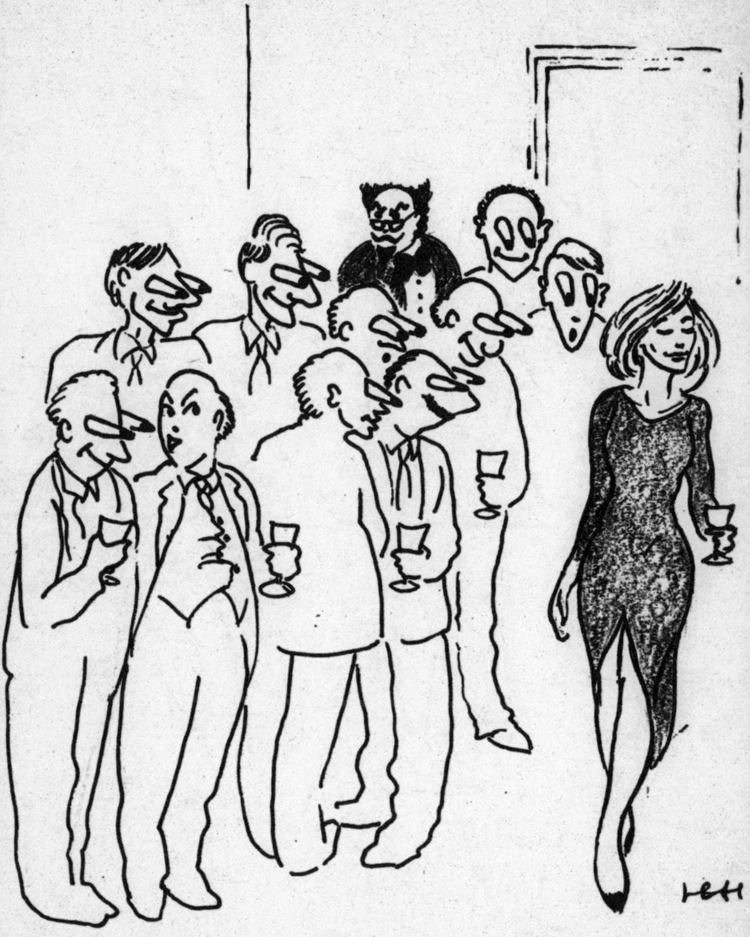

'Don't look now, but there's a psychologist in the room . . .'

Failed in
education . . .

Failed in
business . . .

Failed in
marriage . . .

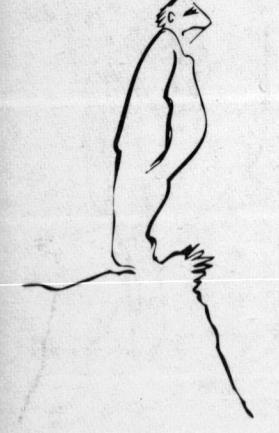

Failed as
a parent . . .

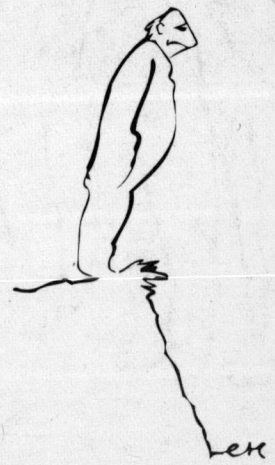

Failed as a lover . . .

Failed as a man . . .

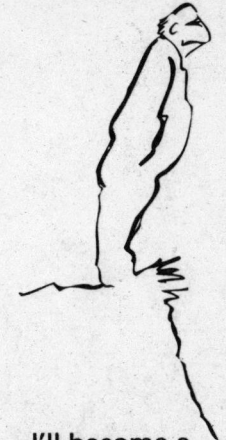

Of course!

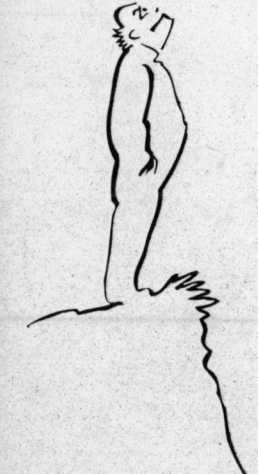

I'll become a sex therapist!

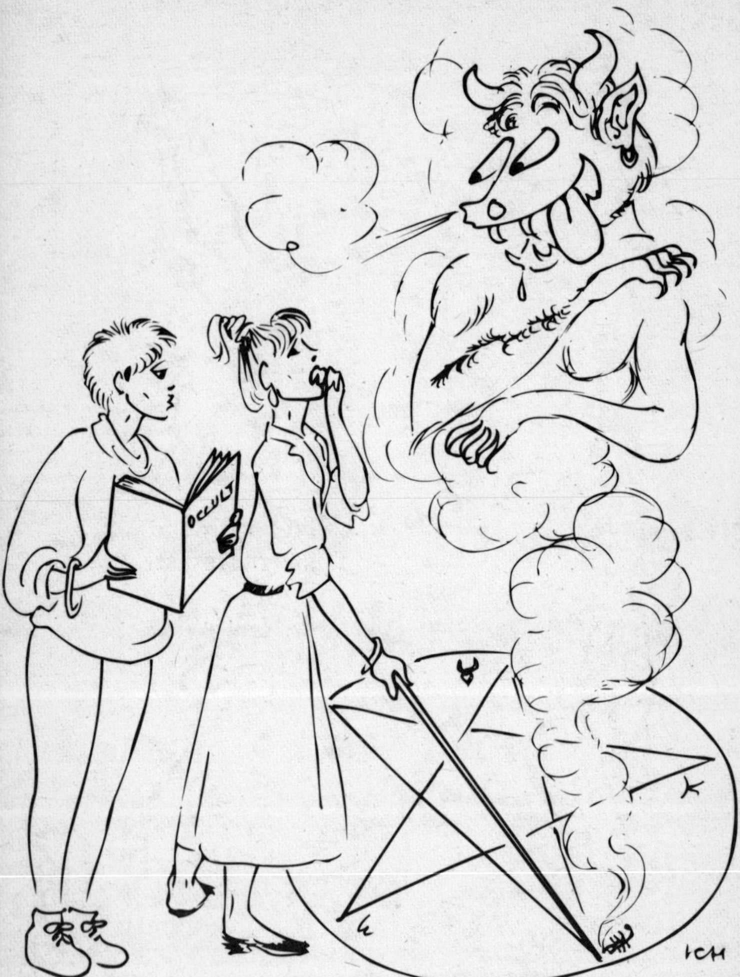
OCCULT
ICH

'Um, no. I think we've summoned up my husband's libido . . .'

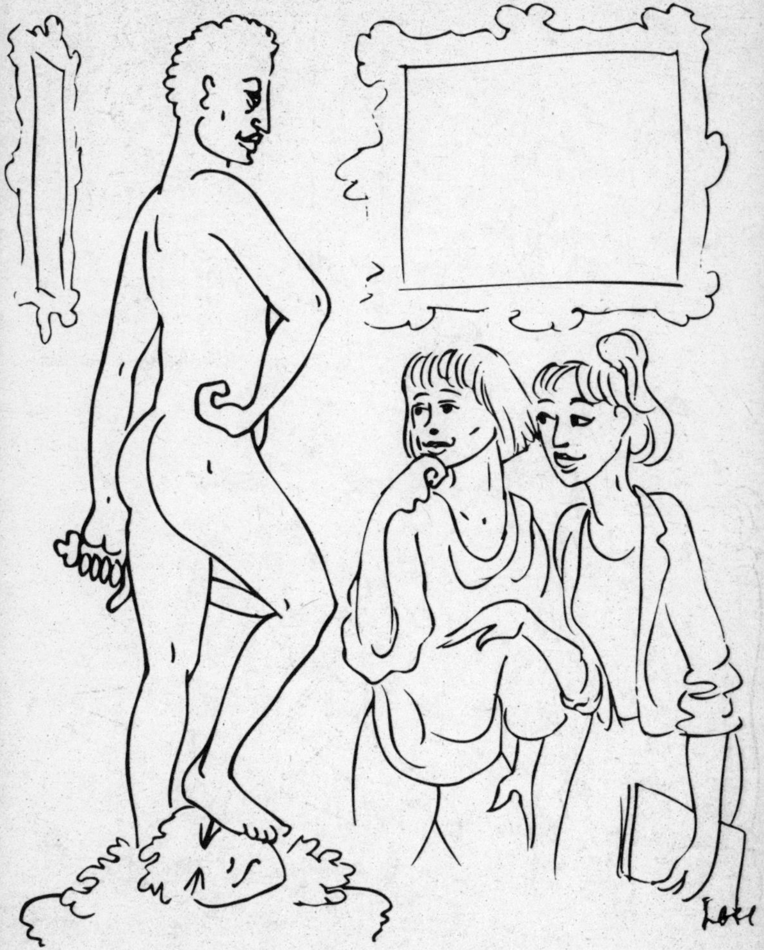

'Obviously done from life; it's tiny . . .'

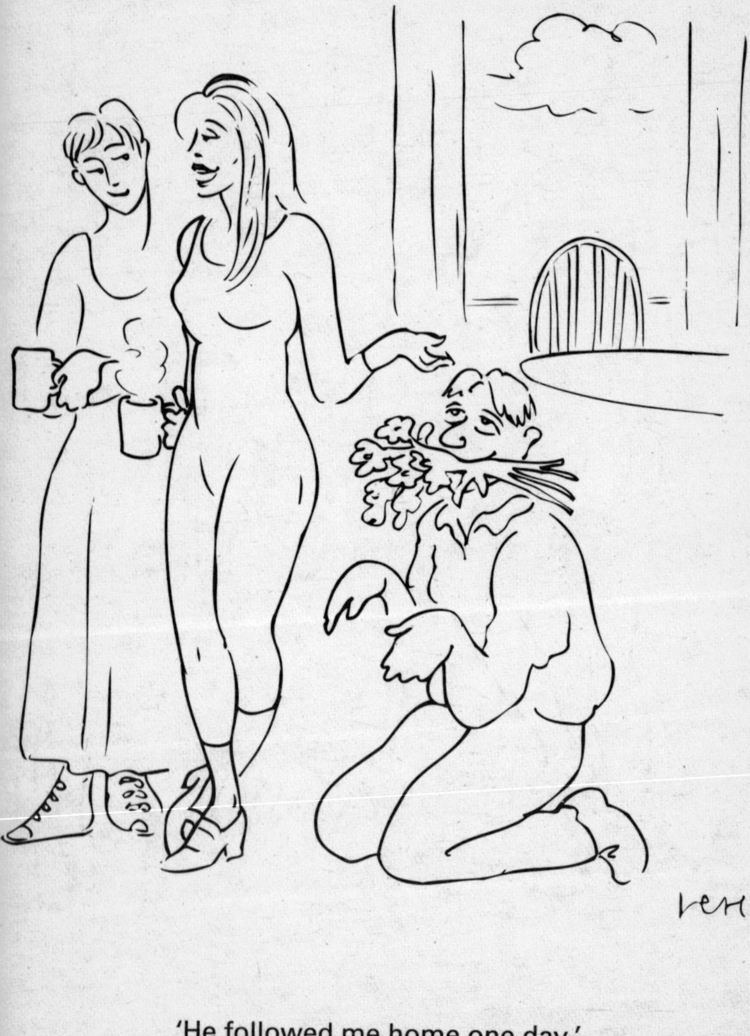

'He followed me home one day.'

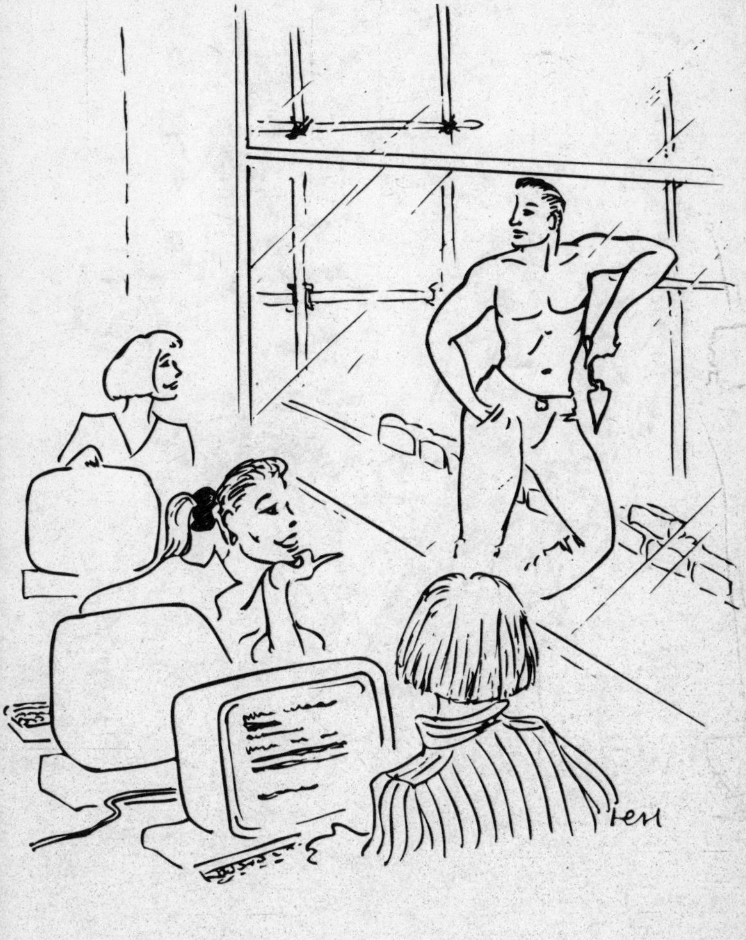

'He's been laying the same ten bricks for a week . . .'

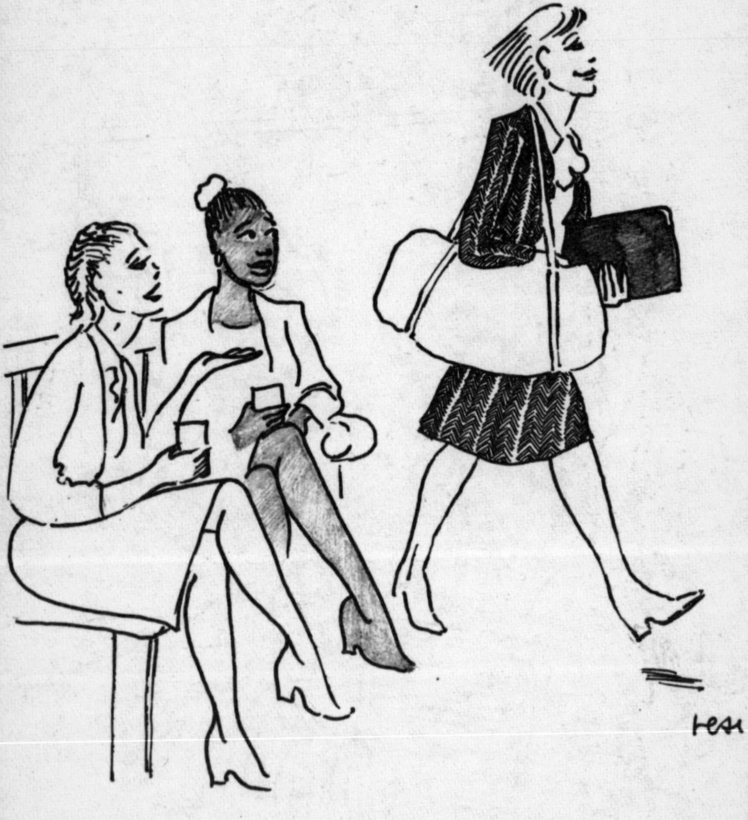

'Waited till she was twenty-eight to sleep with a man, and now she thinks she invented sex . . .'

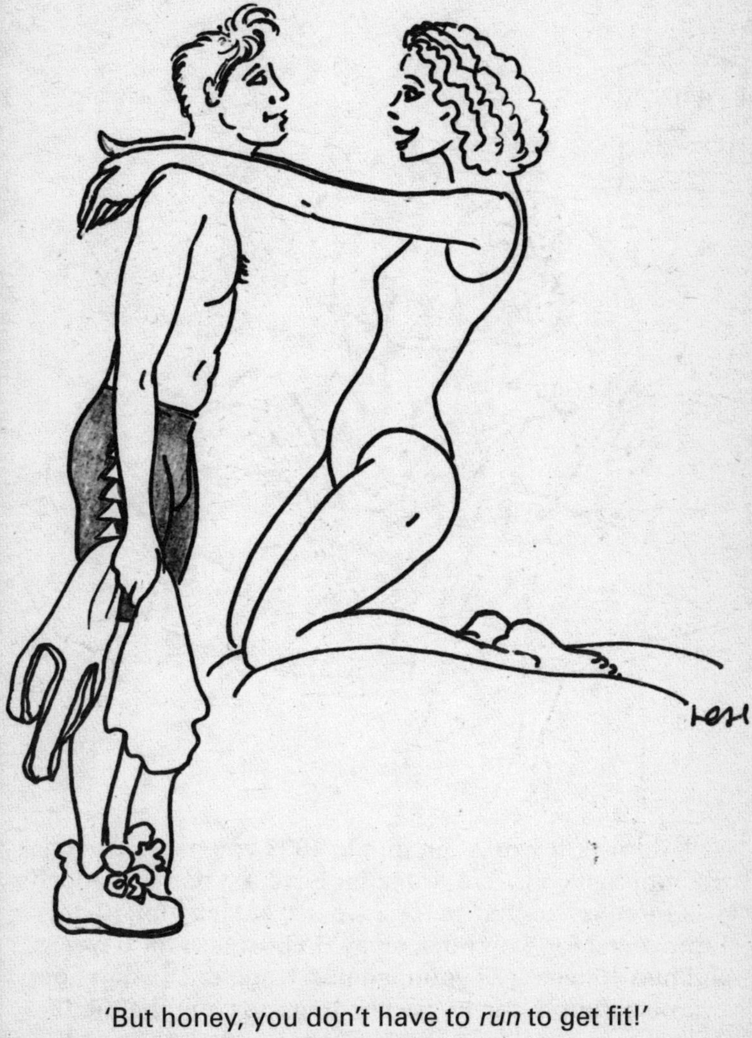

'But honey, you don't have to *run* to get fit!'

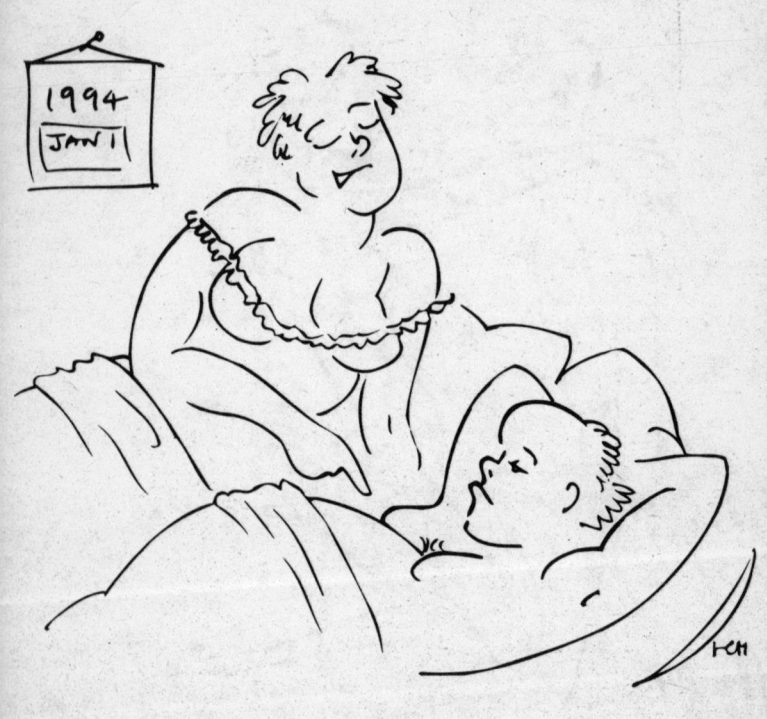

'Well, Romeo. It works out that in 1993 you had a bad back for 2 months, you were drunk for 5 weeks, had a headache for 3 months, toothache for 2 weeks, earache for 10 days, tummyache for 2 months, away on business for 6 weeks, and had 10 weeks of your "special trouble." If I don't get some action this year, *you're* going to be embalmed!'

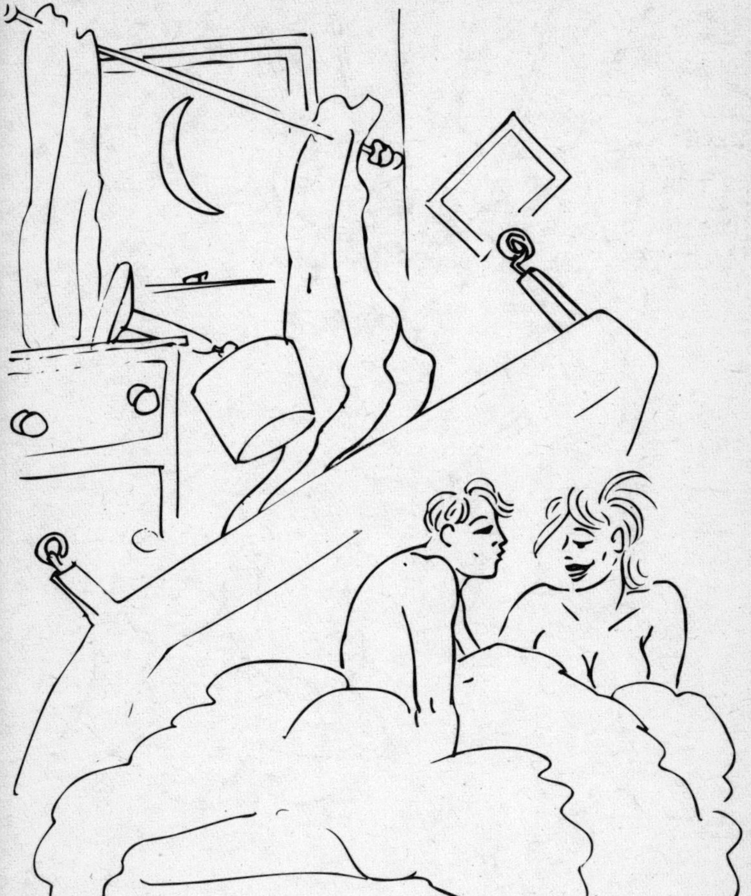
LCH

'Under the circumstances, sweetheart, that's a rather silly question . . .'

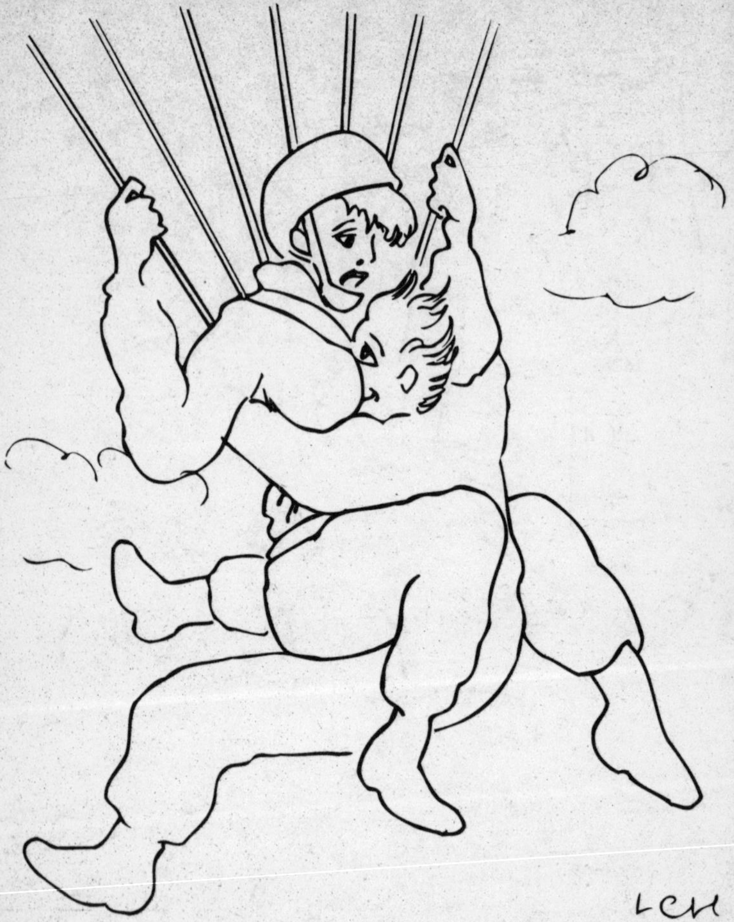
LCH

'I still think you forgot it on purpose!'

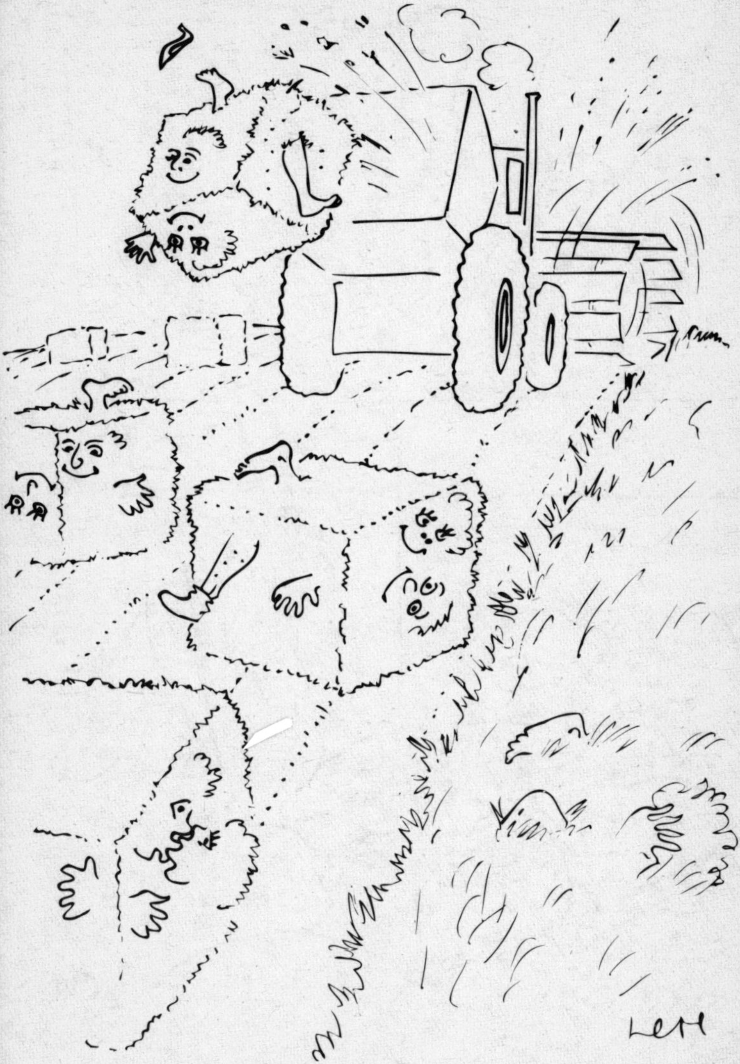

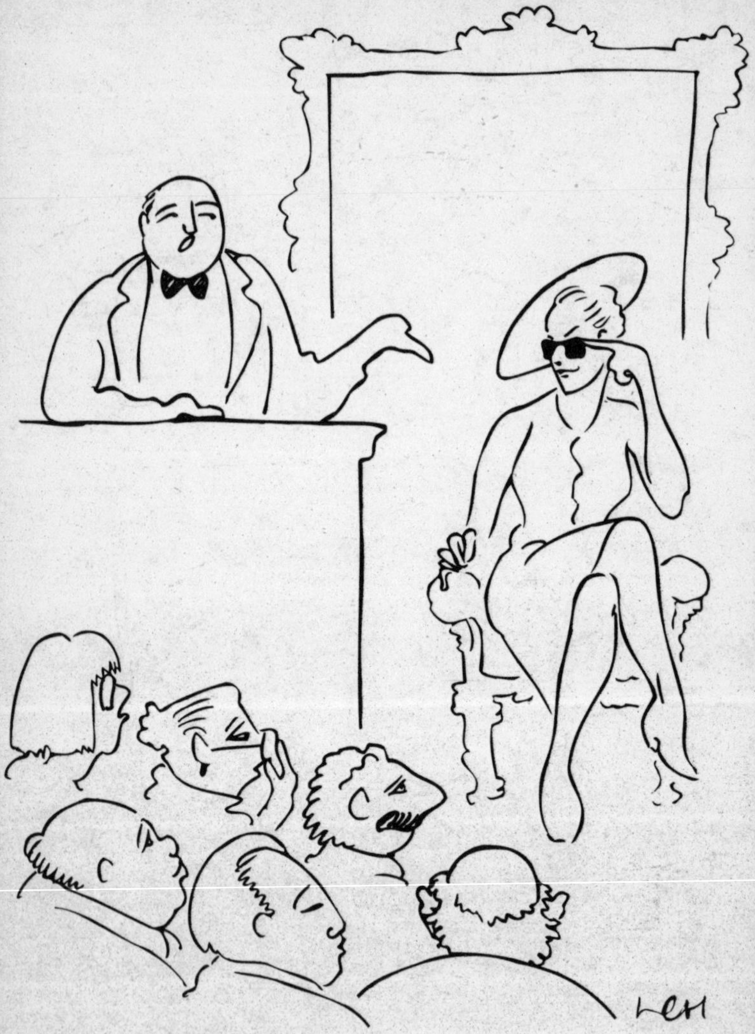

'Lot 24. The property of a gentleman.'

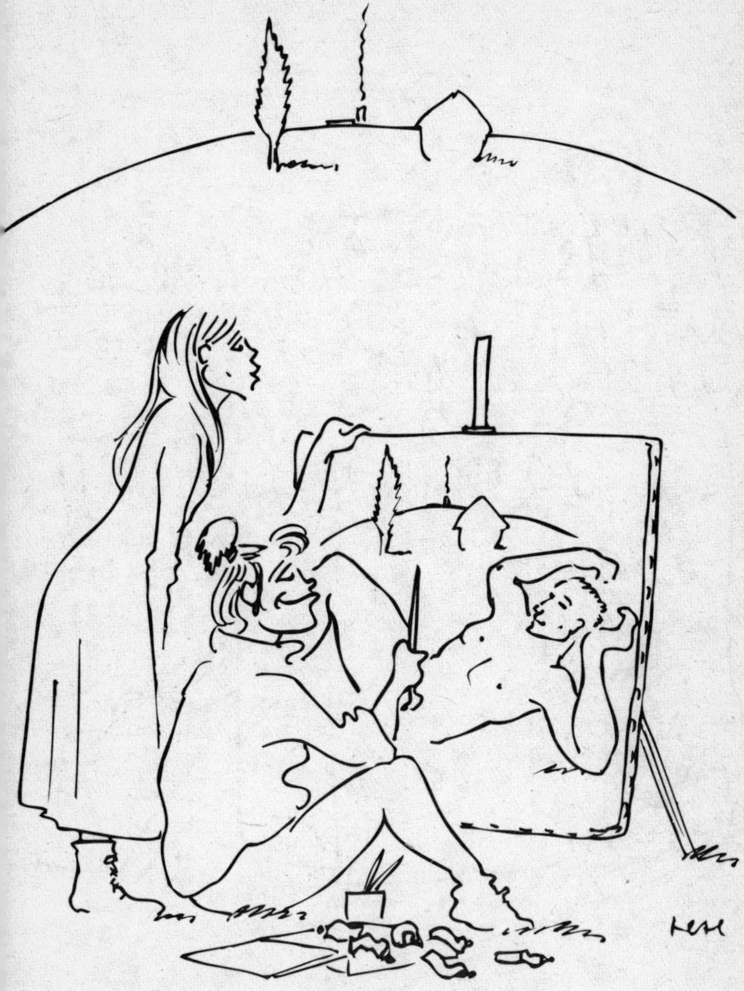

'Honestly, Prunella, you've got the most wonderful imagination!'

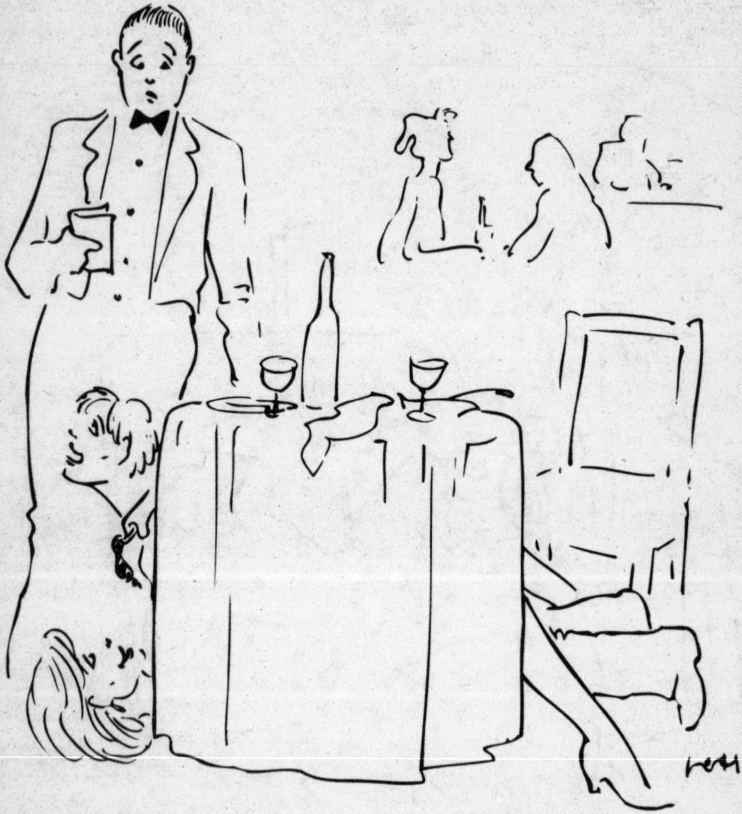

'We noticed there was no service charge . . .'

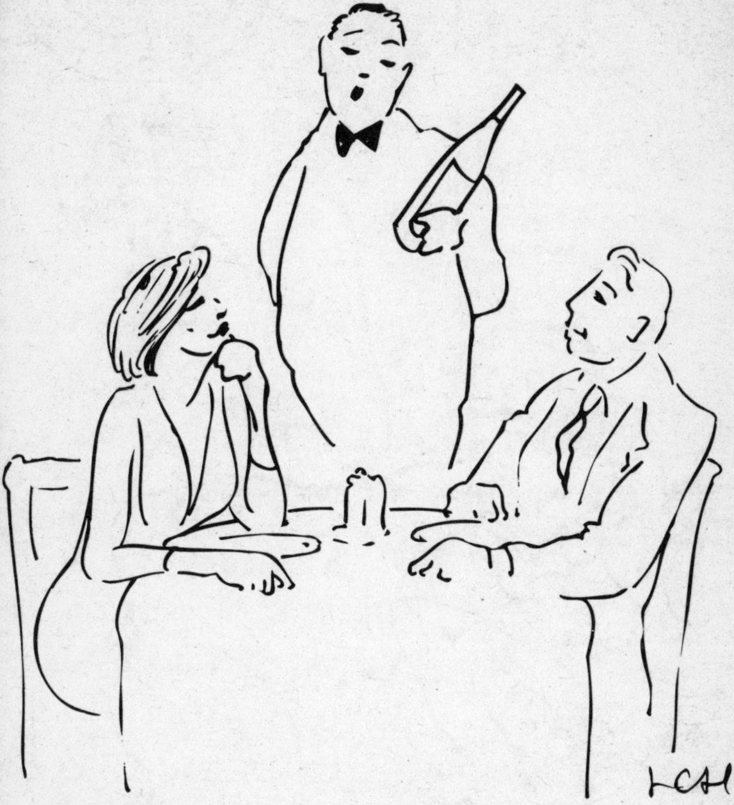
LCH

'For what Sir has in mind, perhaps three triple gins would be more appropriate?'

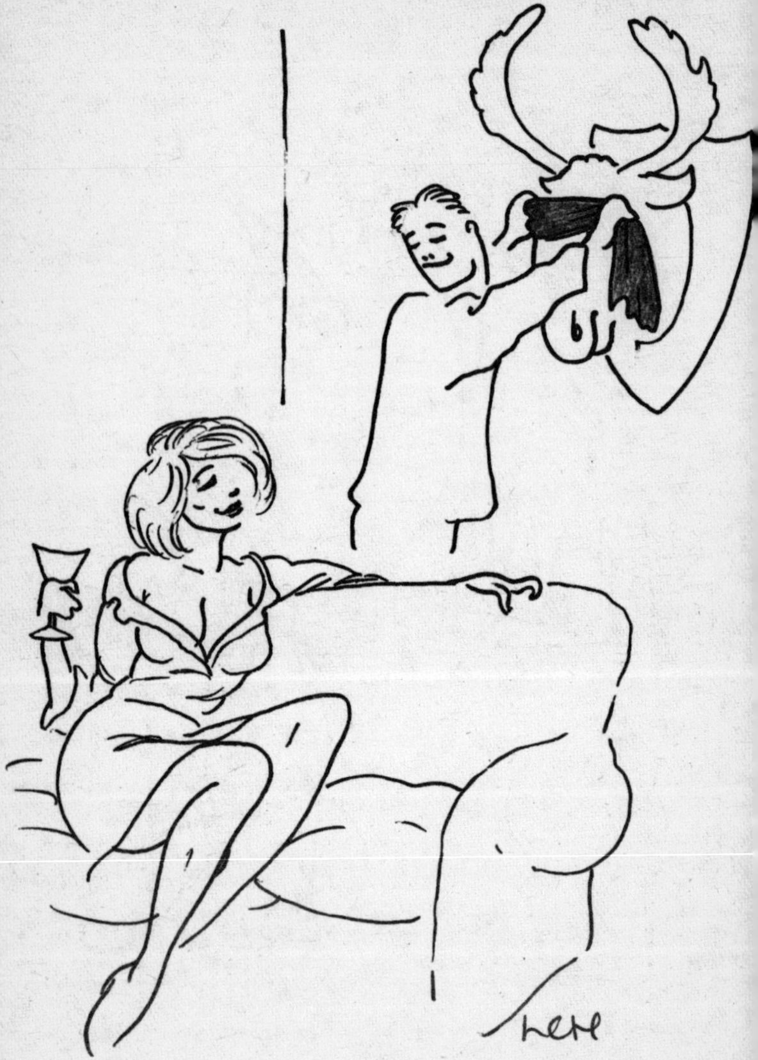

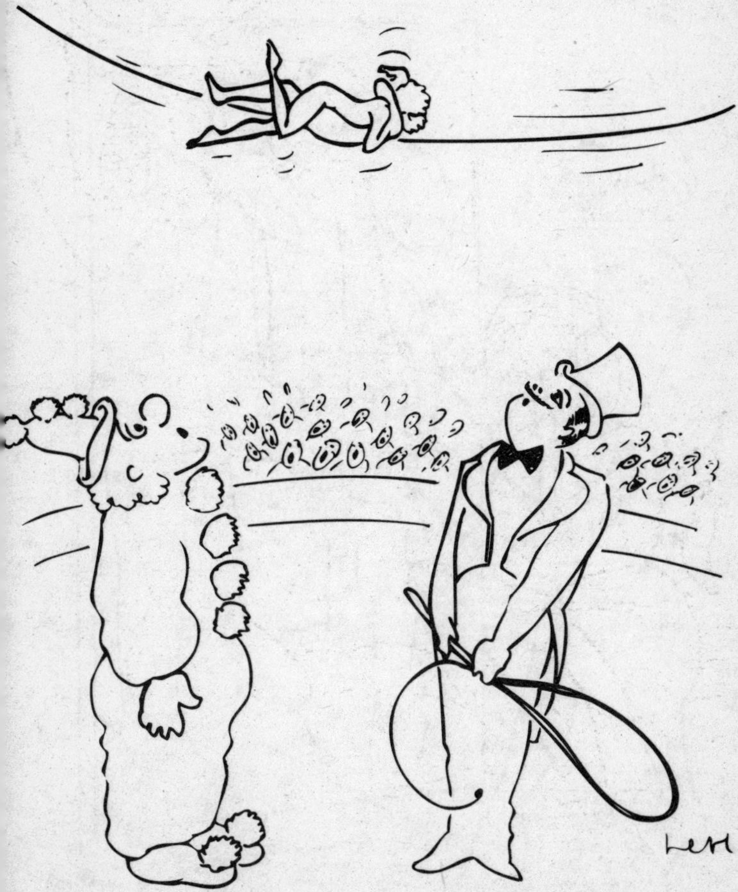

'But you have to admire their balance.'

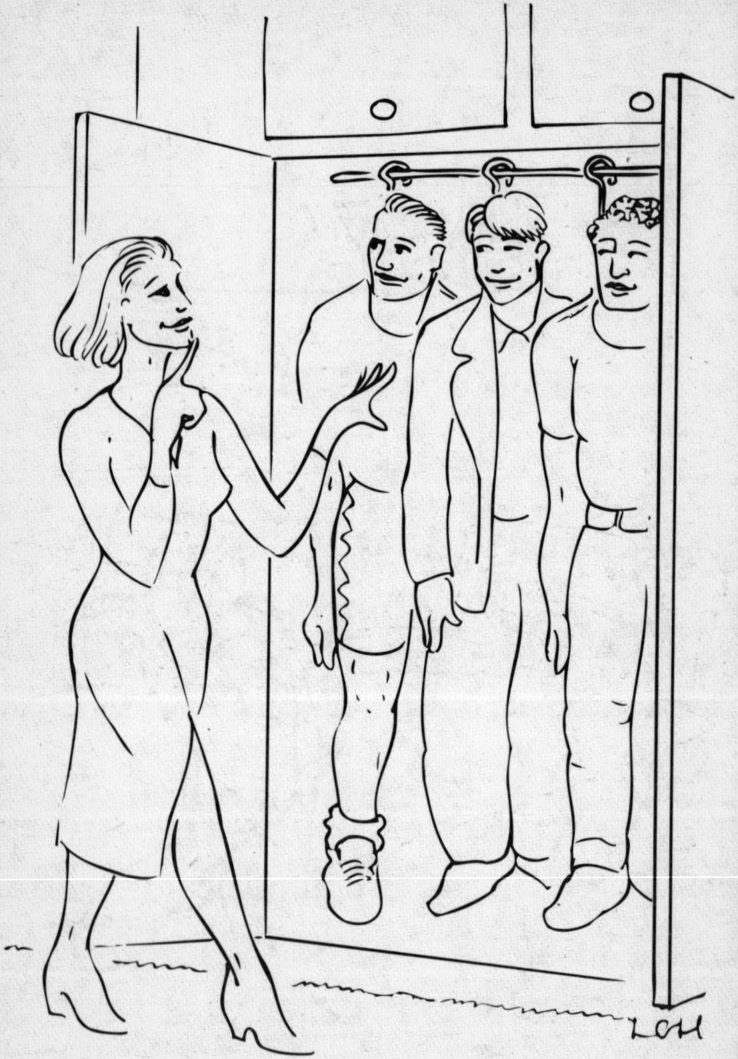
LCH

'The ultimate fashion accessory . . .'

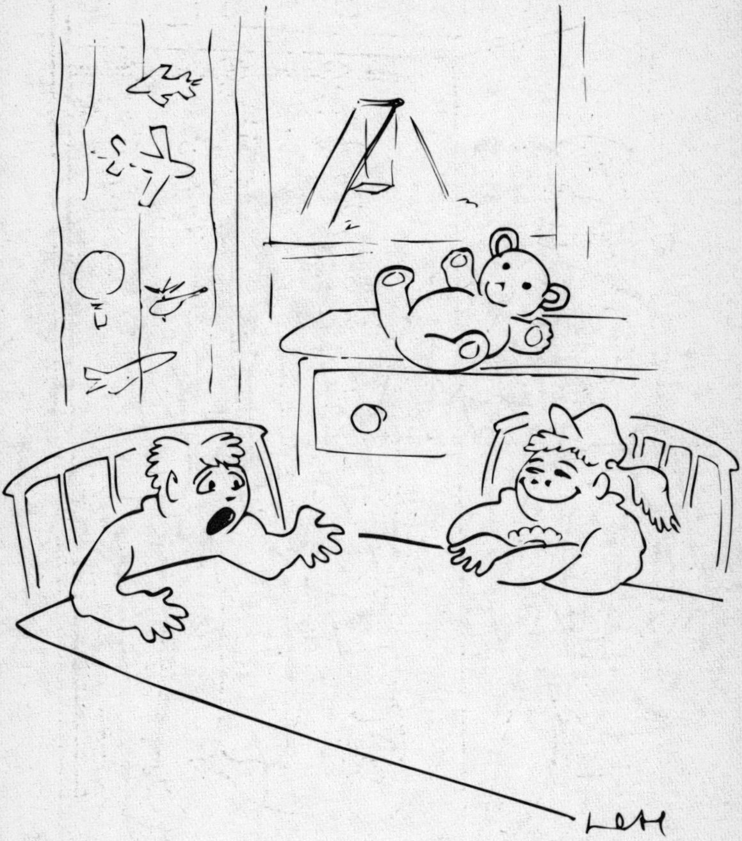

'But I can't even *spell* "pre-nuptial"!'

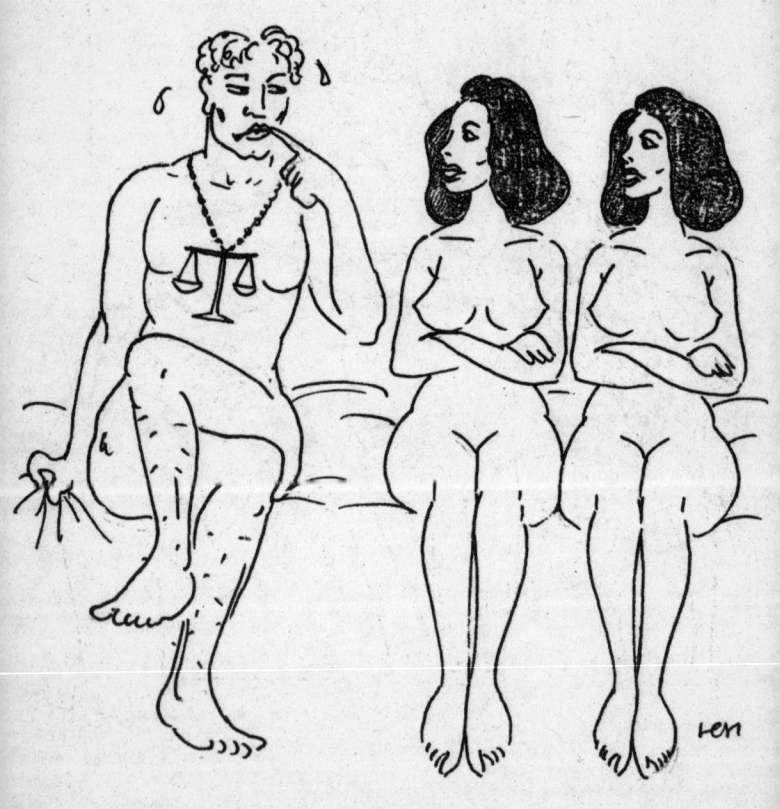

'Oh, *do* make up your mind!'

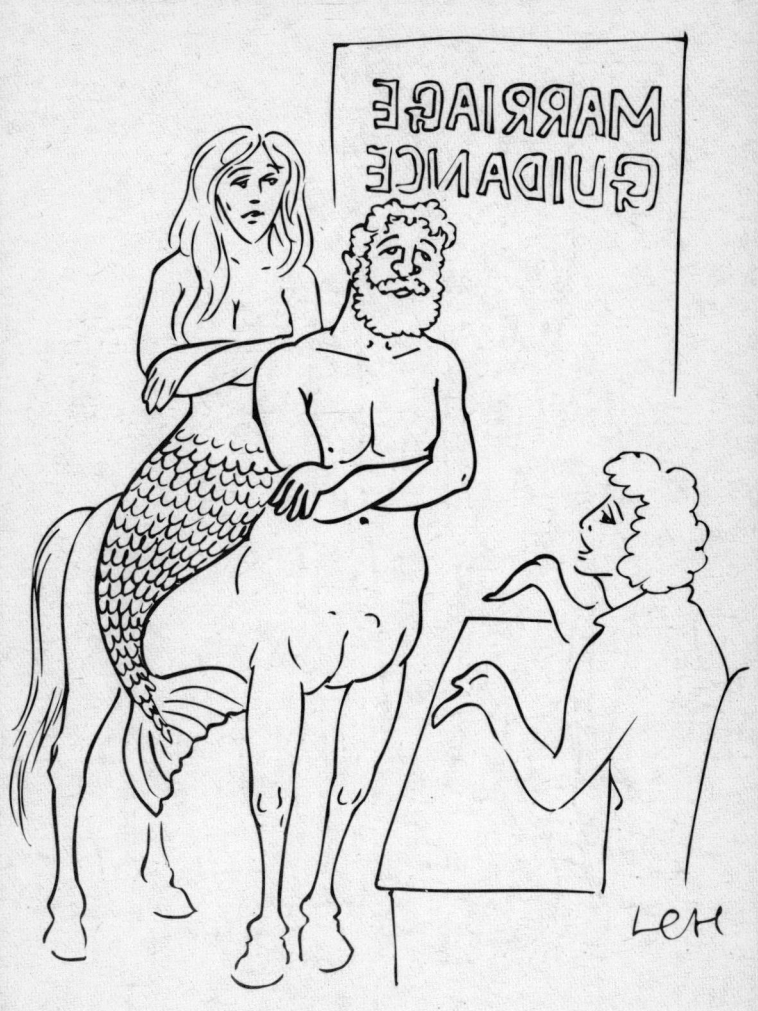

'Good relationships often need more than just
traditional values . . .'

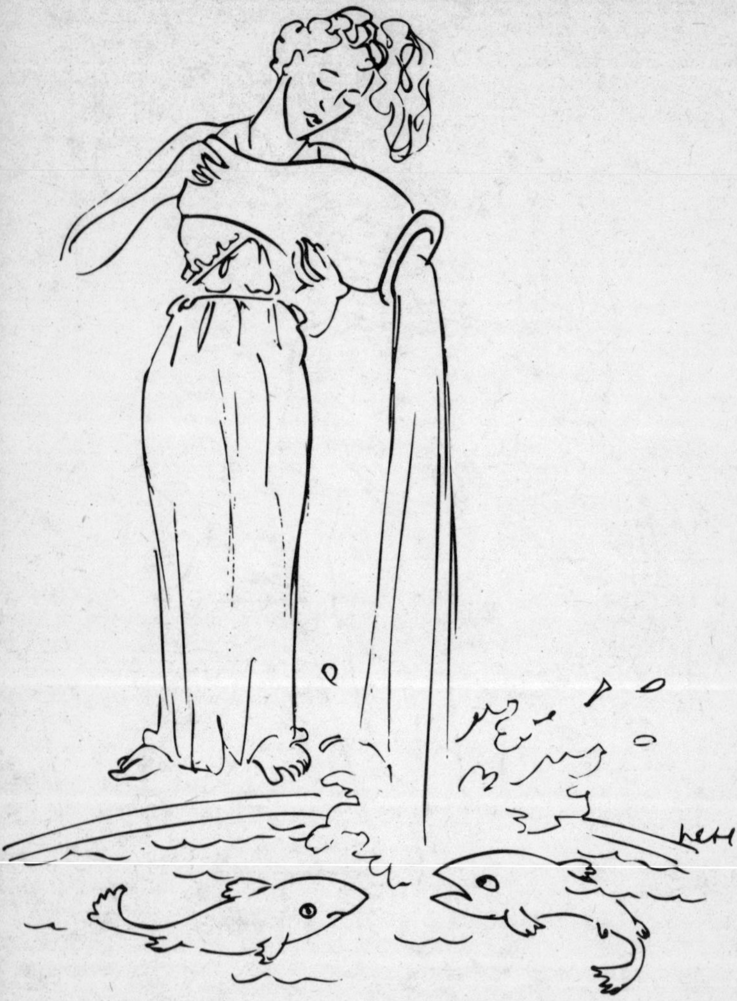

'I know she's sensuous, she's traditional, but I'd still rather have Champagne . . .'

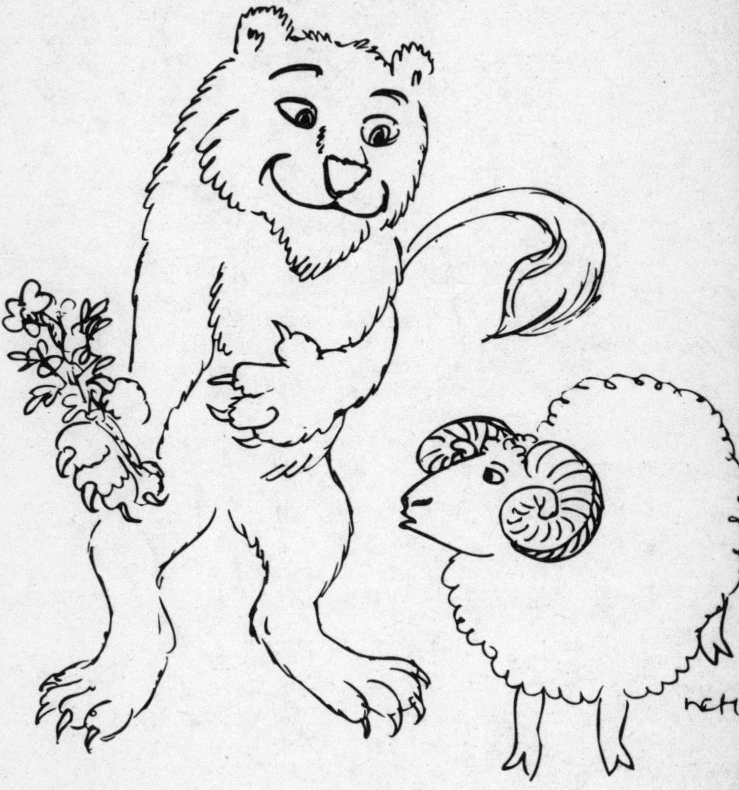

'Why d'you always give me *mint?*'

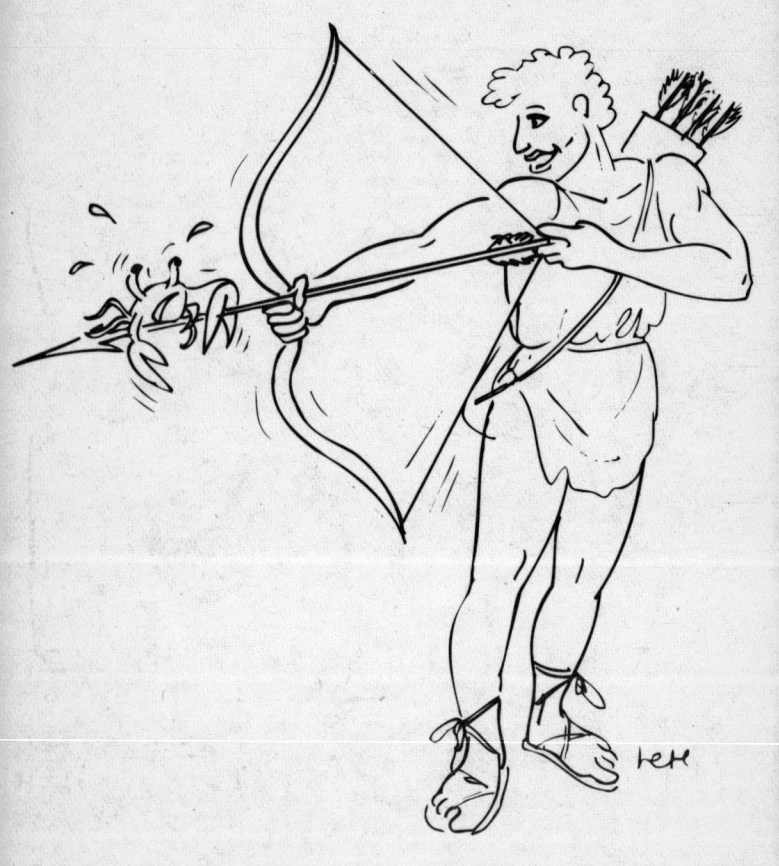

'Trust me! It's quicker than walking!'

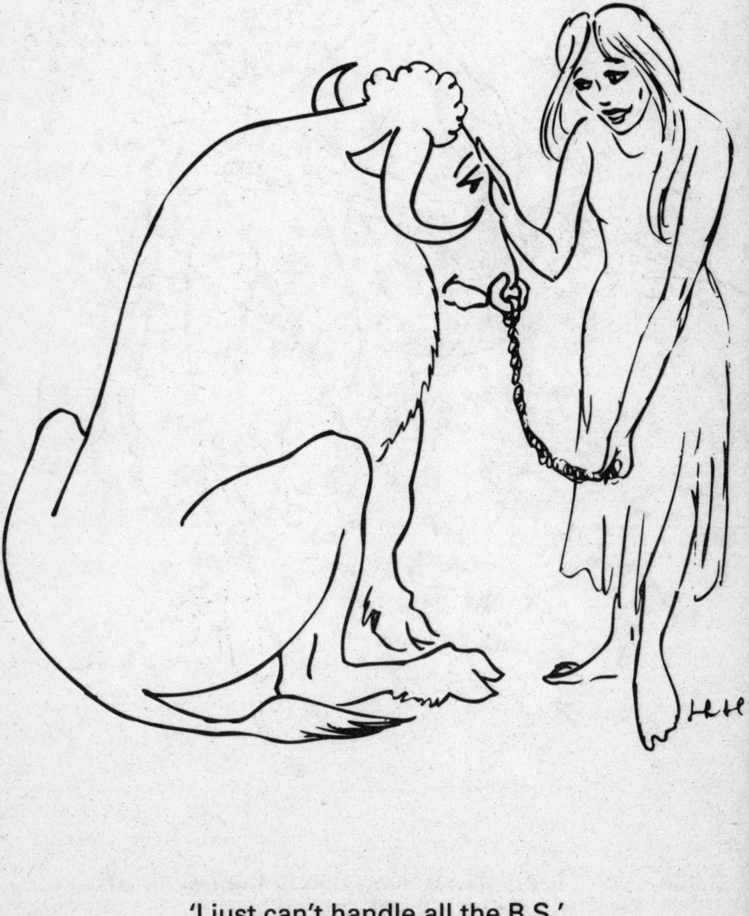

'I just can't handle all the B.S.'

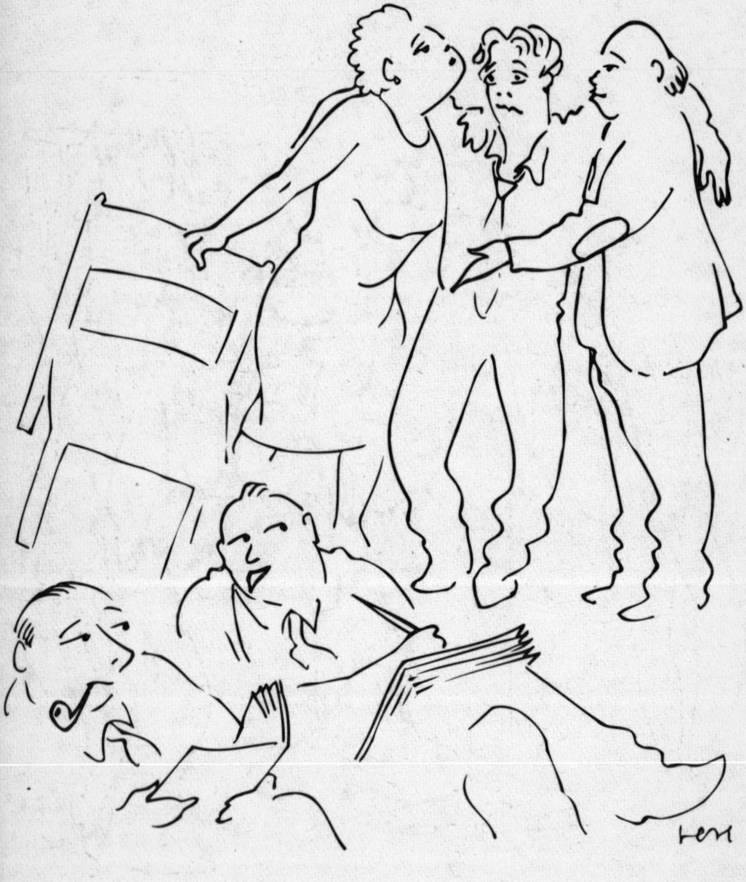

'I see young Frobisher's been taking the Lower Sixth for Sex Education again . . .'

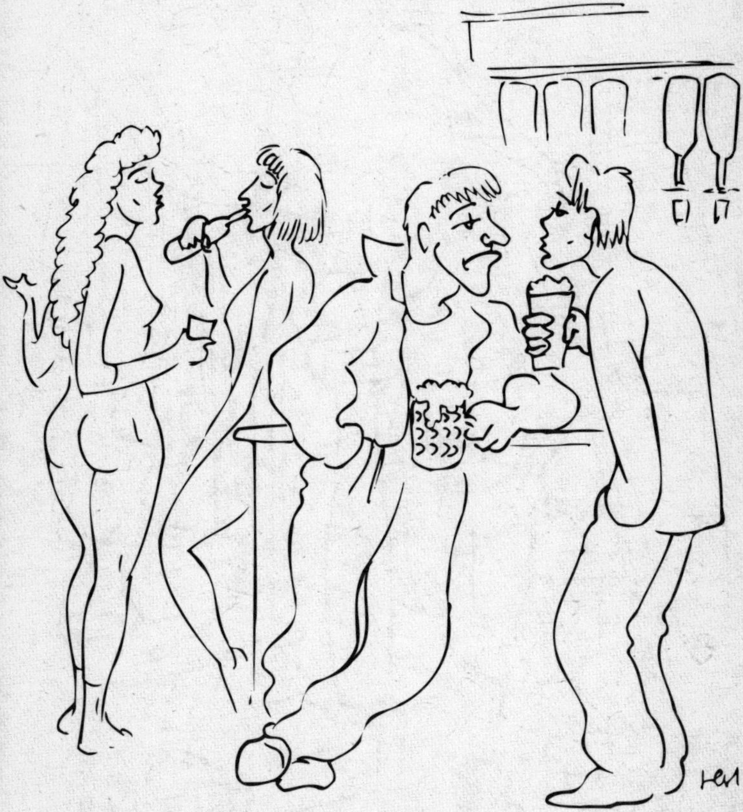

'Nah, I know I can always pick up a pint . . .'

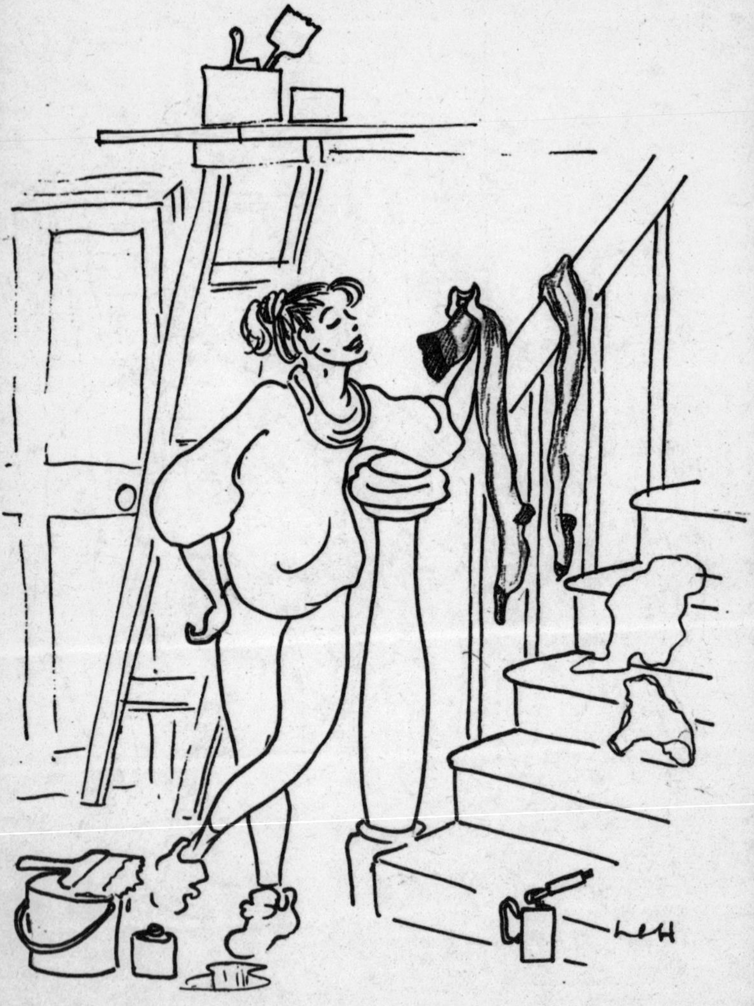
LeH

'Darling, I asked you for a *paint* stripper . . .'

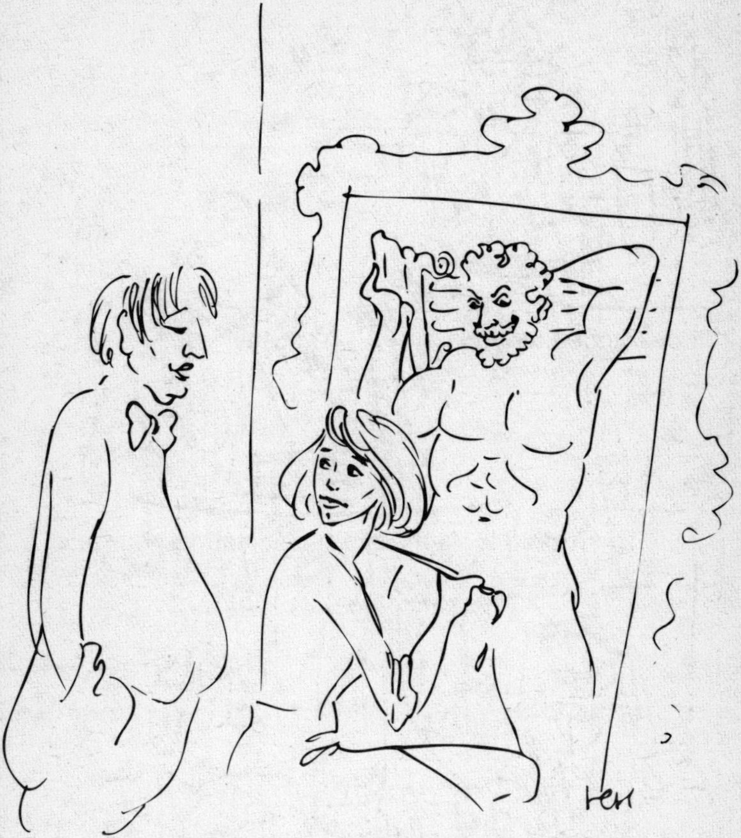

‘I suppose that’s one woman’s concept of restoration, Ms Jones.’

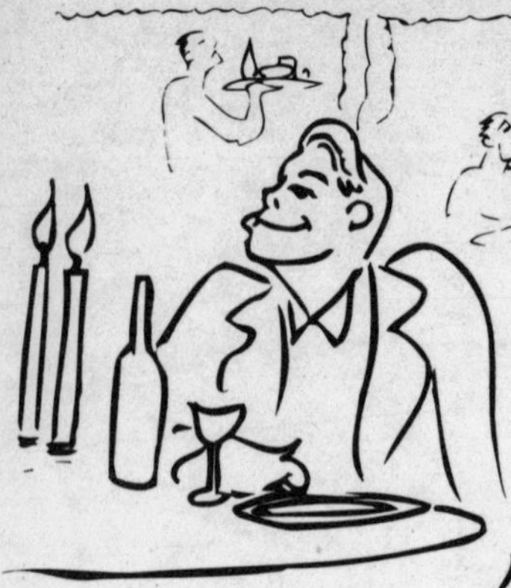

'I'm bewitched by you . . .'

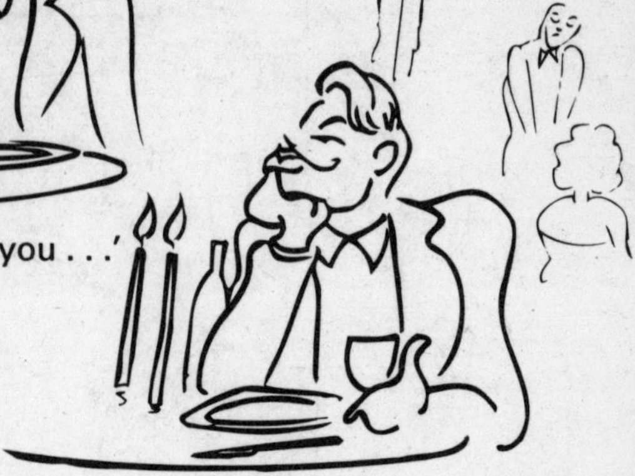

'The more I look, the more fascinating your face . . .'

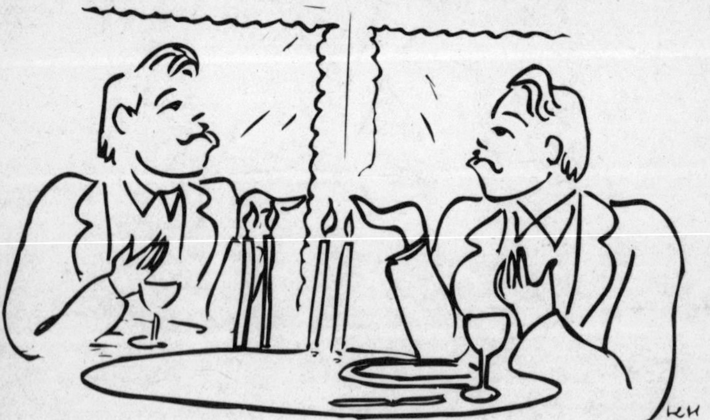

'But – well, we just can't go on meeting like this . . .'

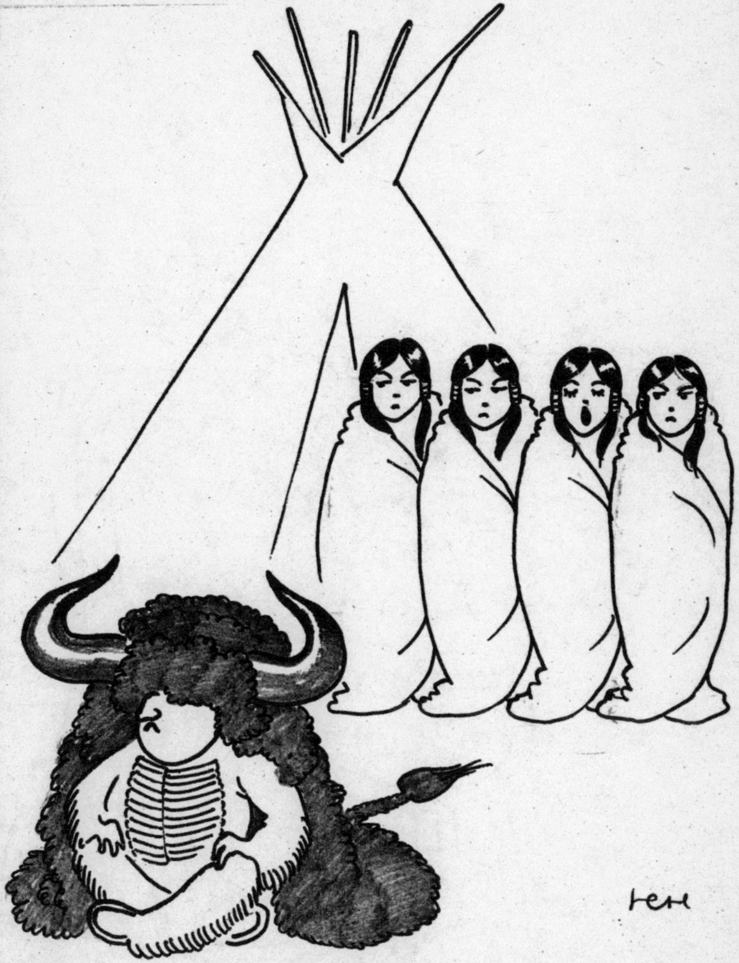

'Patience, Buffalo Wallow Women, he's just getting his confidence up for us . . .'

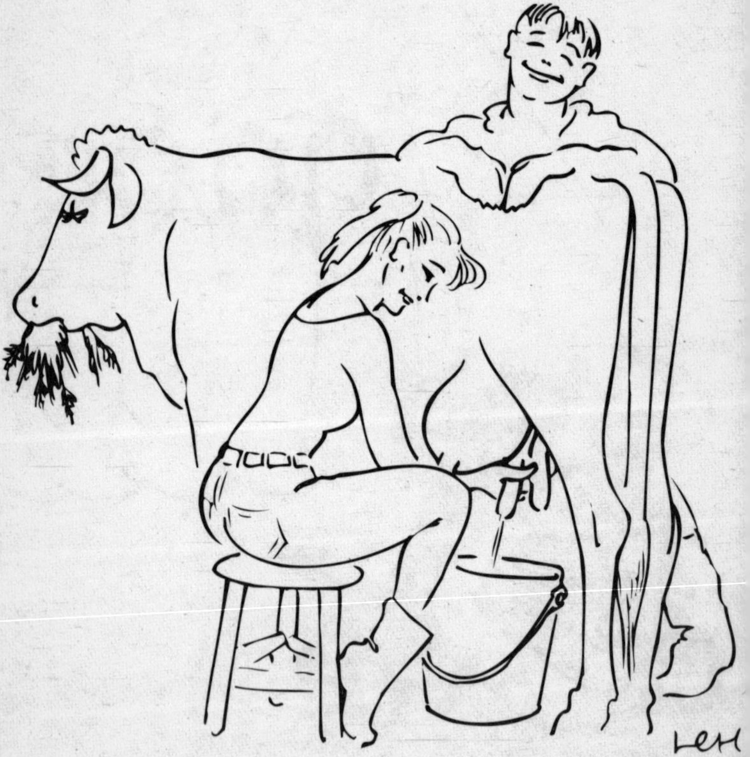

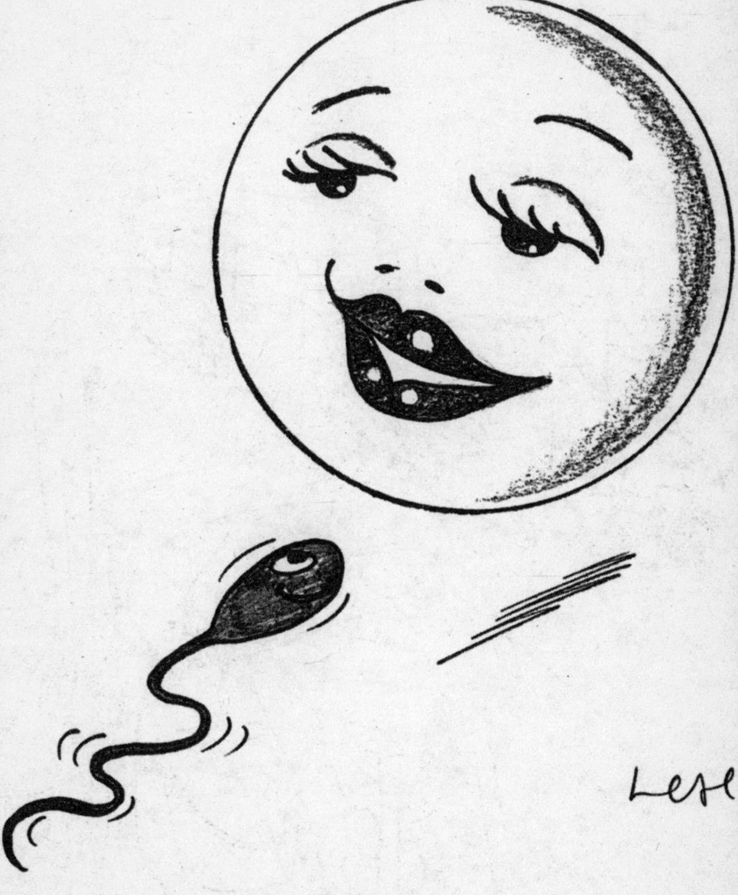
Lete

'Is that some DNA in your zygote,
or are you just pleased to see me?'

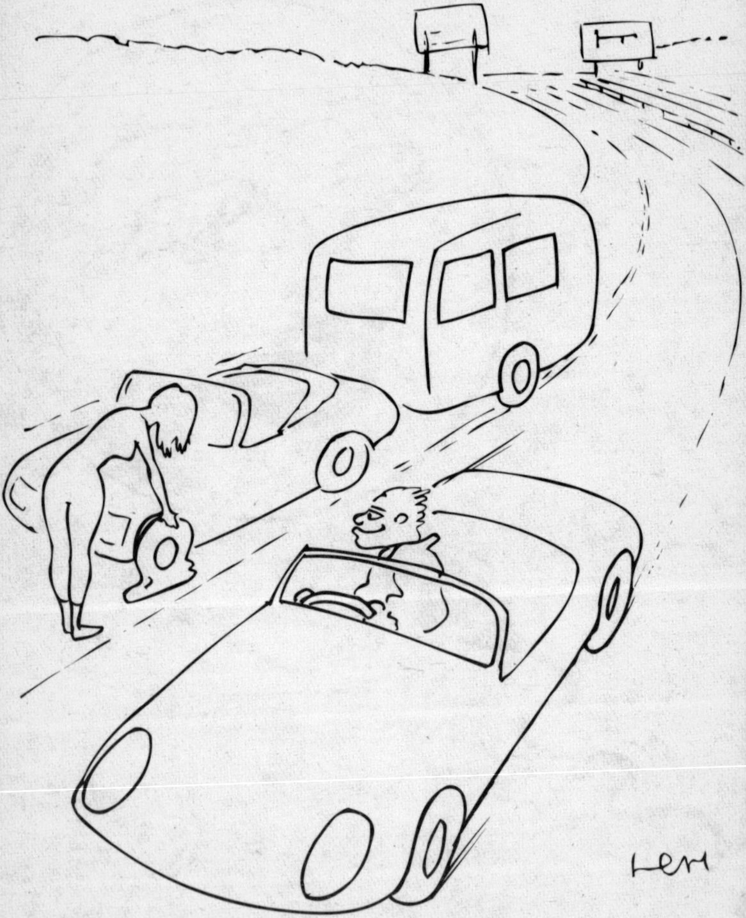

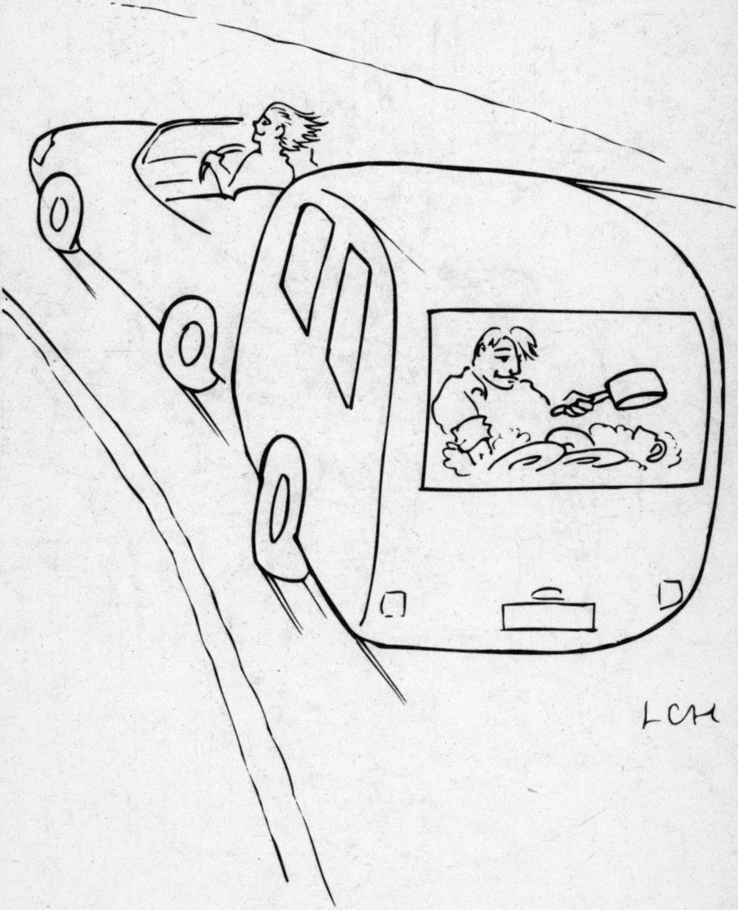

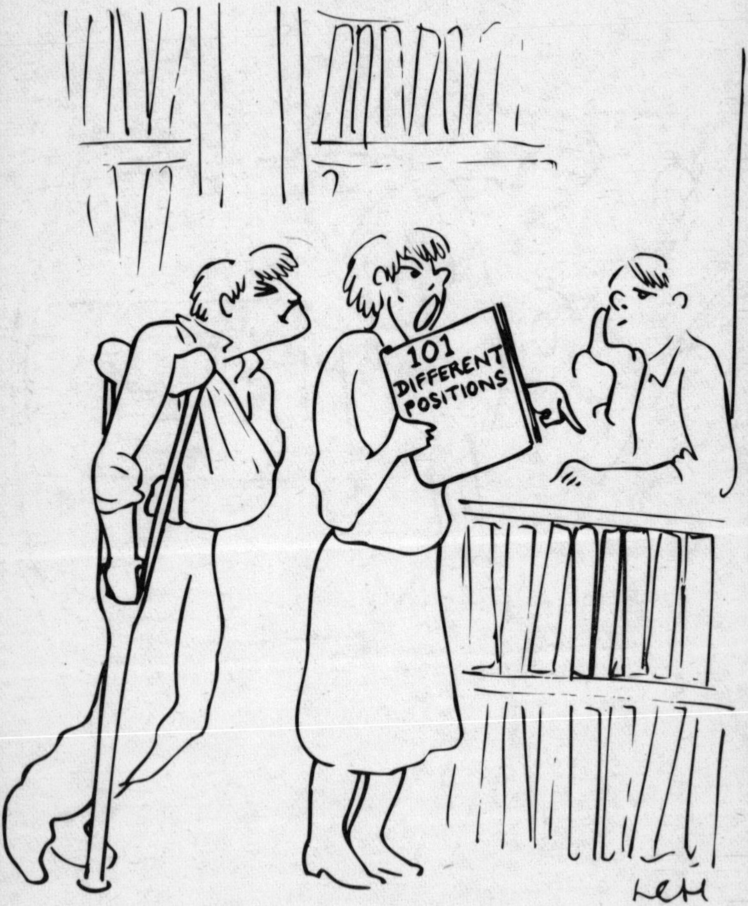
101
DIFFERENT
POSITIONS

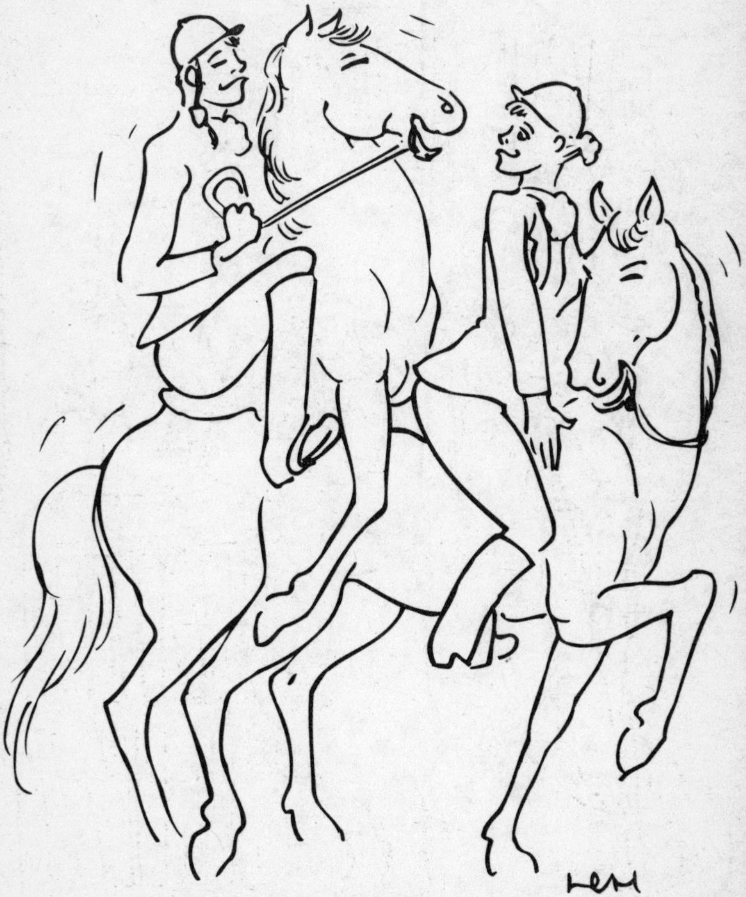

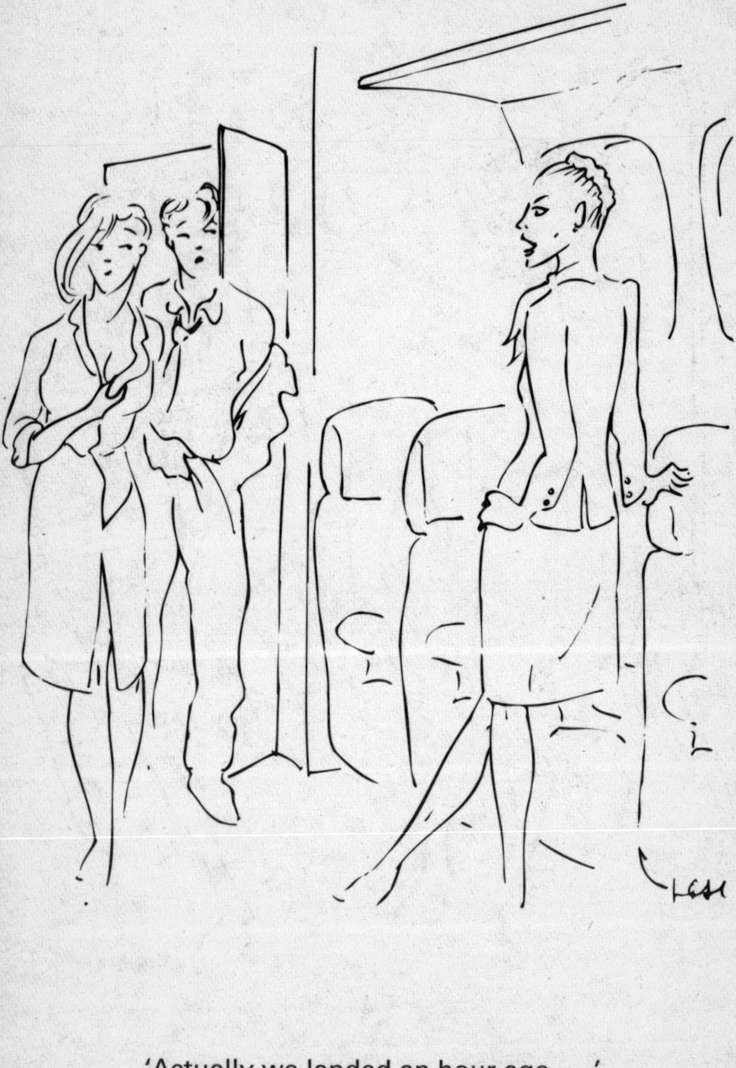

'Actually we landed an hour ago . . .'

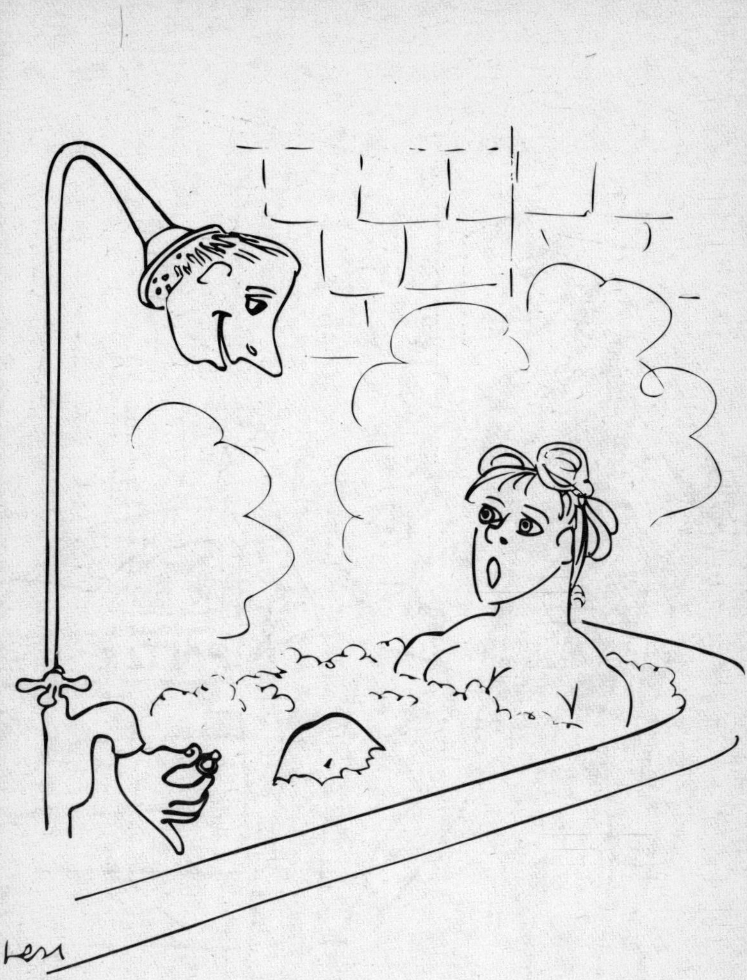

'I told you I was persistent, Mildred!'

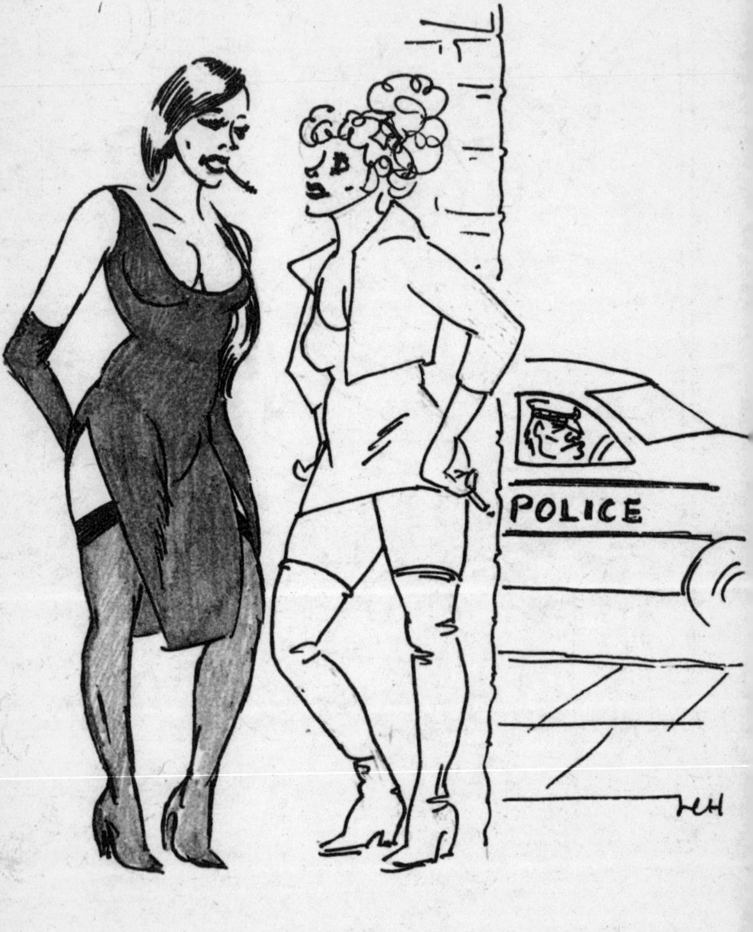

POLICE

'No, love. The Judge always dresses like that, so he can pick me up without him getting picked up . . .'

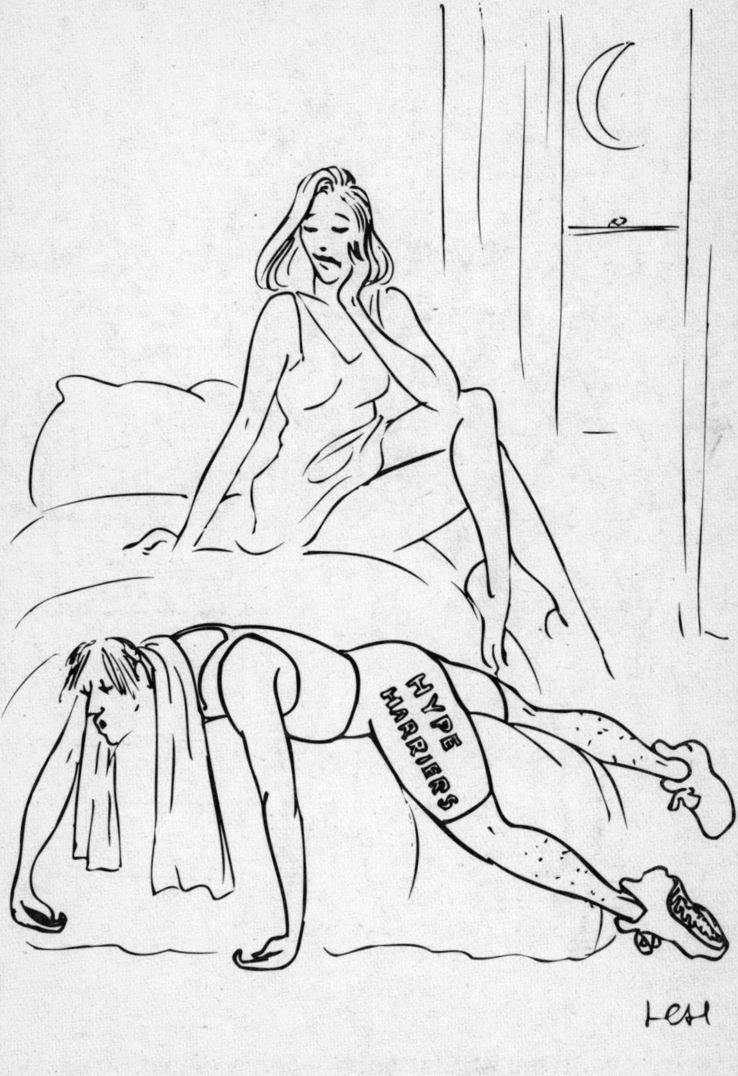
HYPE
HARRIERS

'I see I can expect another perfect night of rest . . . again.'

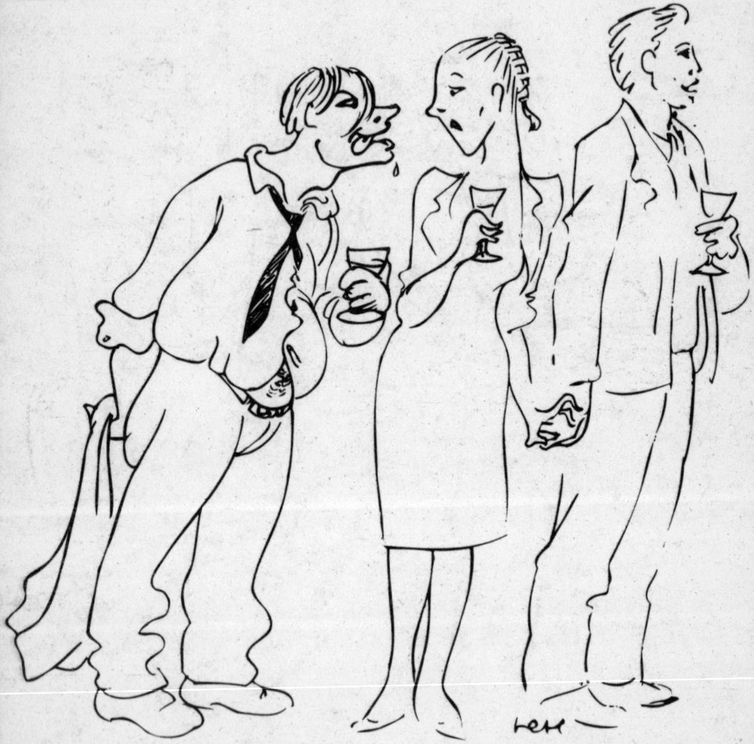

'Do the words "Equal Opportunities" mean anything to you?'

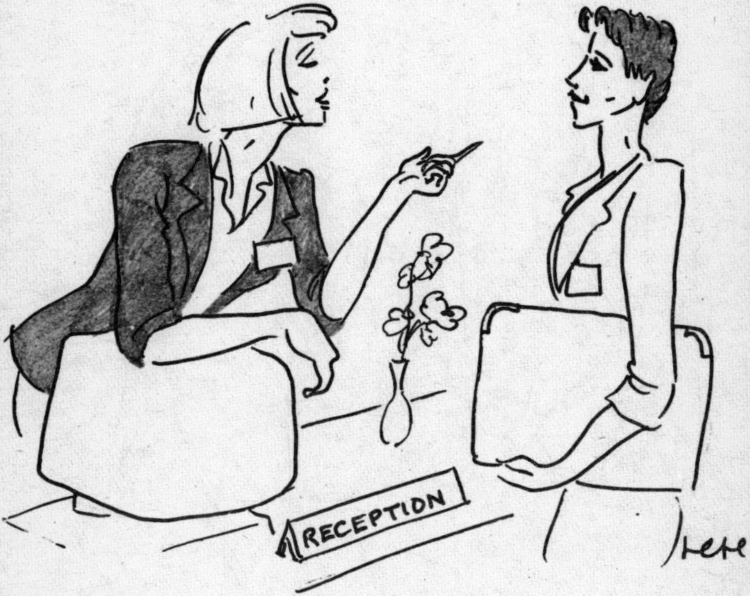
RECEPTION
Irene

'Yes, you go past the chunky hunk with the tan, right by the Mel Gibson look-alike, up the stairs by the guy with the gorgeous eyes, and it's the door next to the one with the incredible bum . . .'

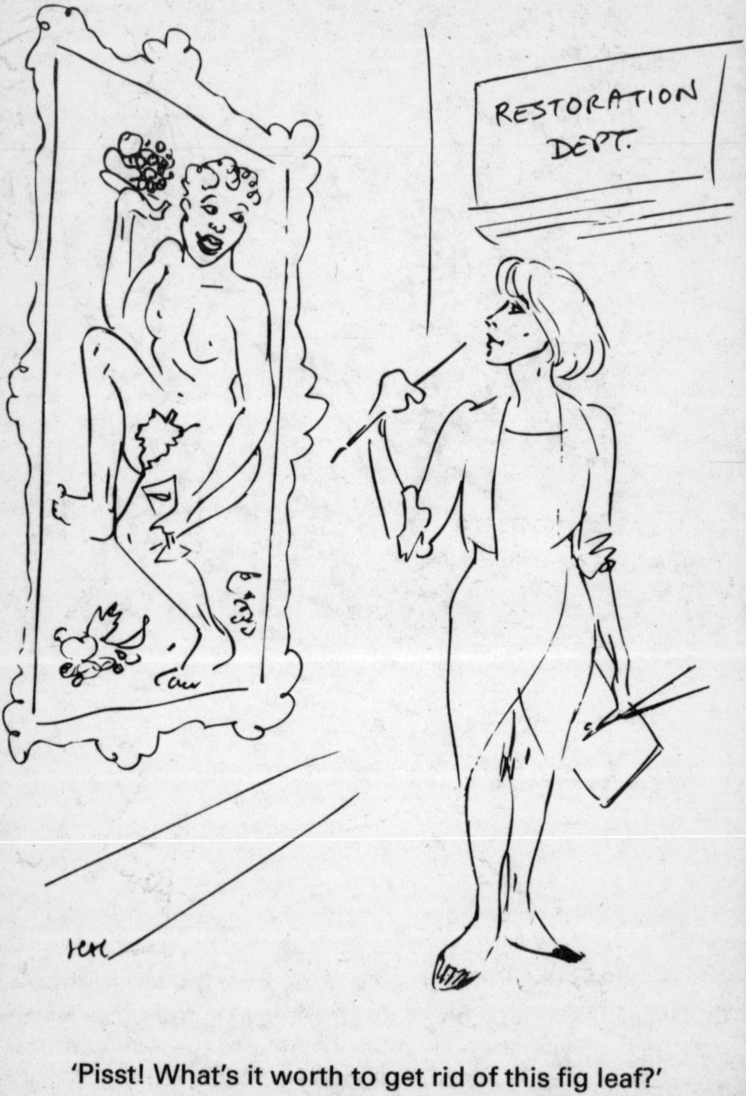
RESTORATION
DEPT.

'Pisst! What's it worth to get rid of this fig leaf?'

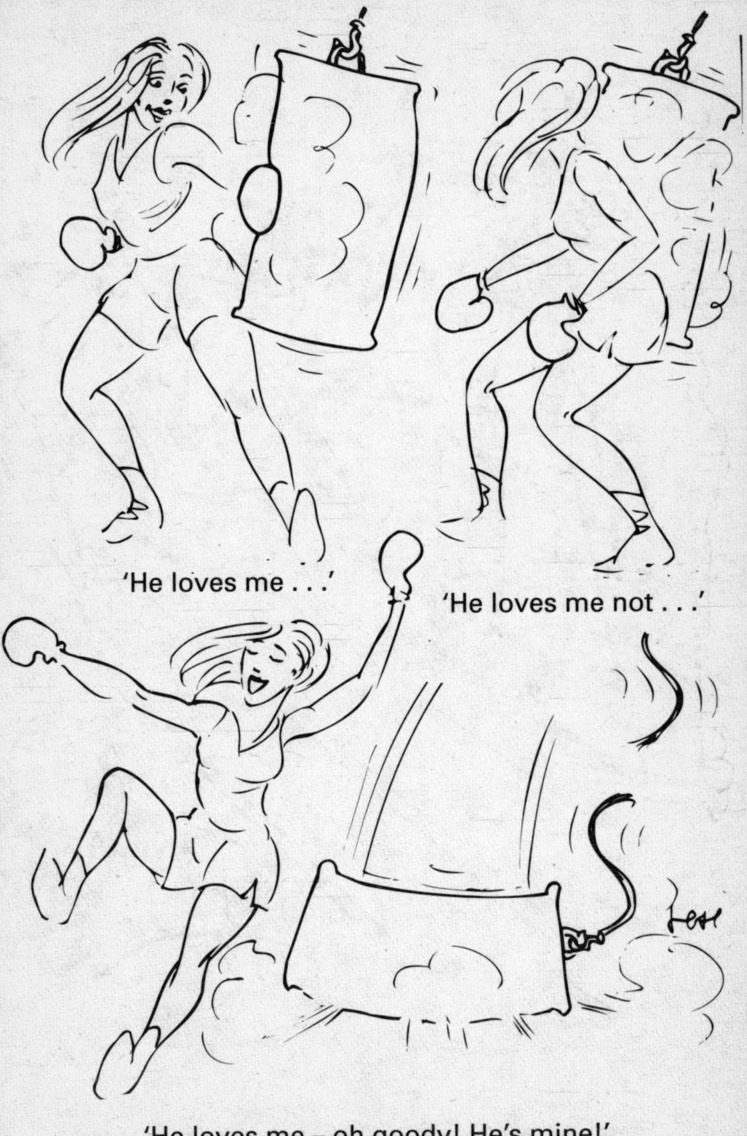

'He loves me . . .'

'He loves me not . . .'

'He loves me – oh goody! He's mine!'

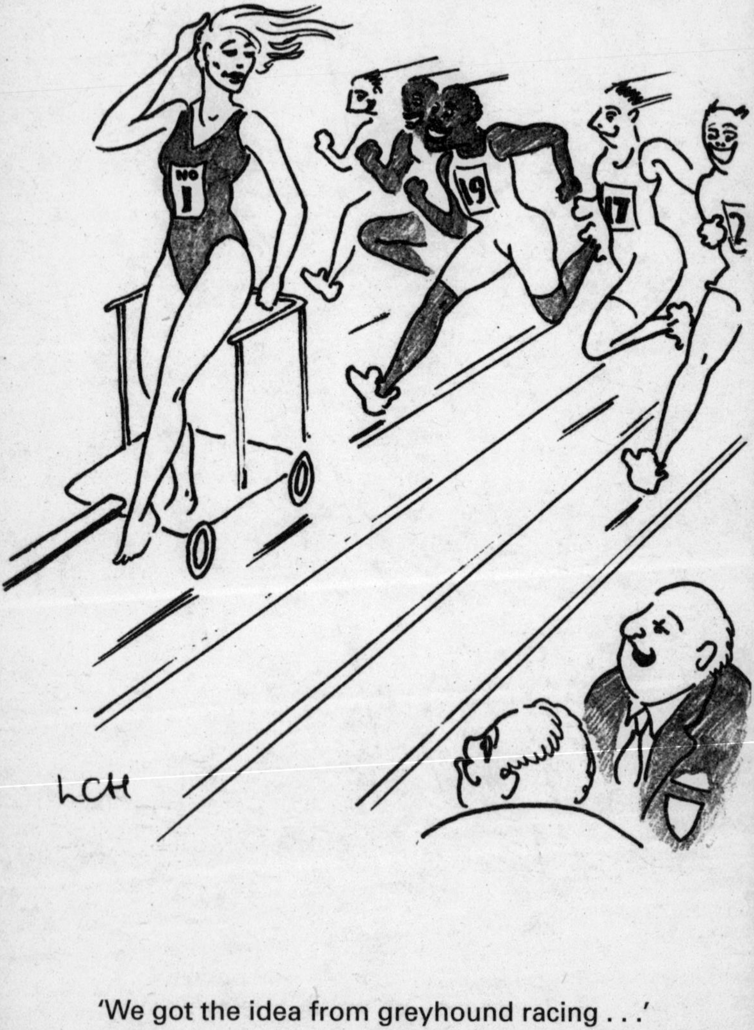
NO
1
19
17
2
LCH

'We got the idea from greyhound racing . . .'

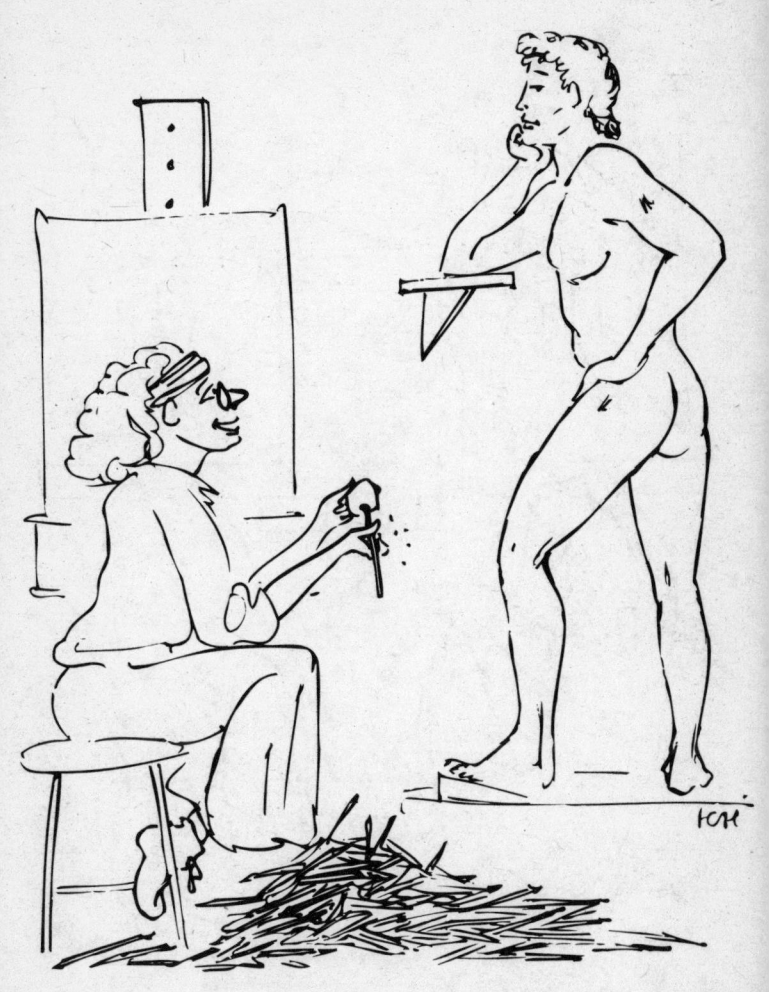

'First, I'll just sharpen a few pencils . . .'

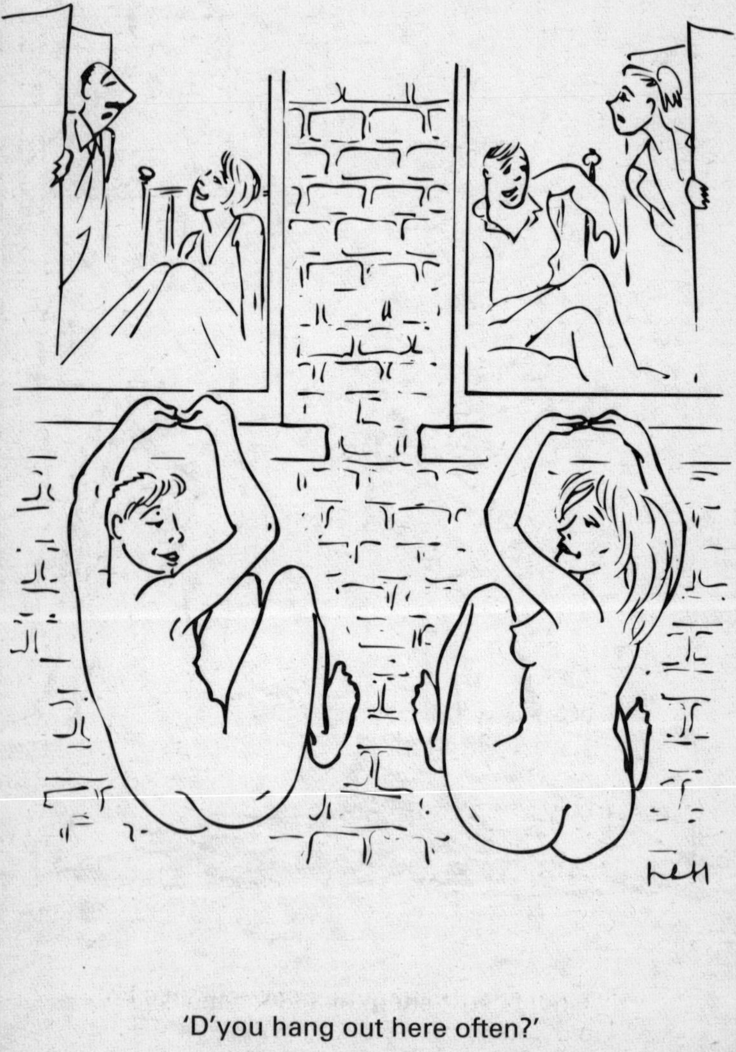

'D'you hang out here often?'

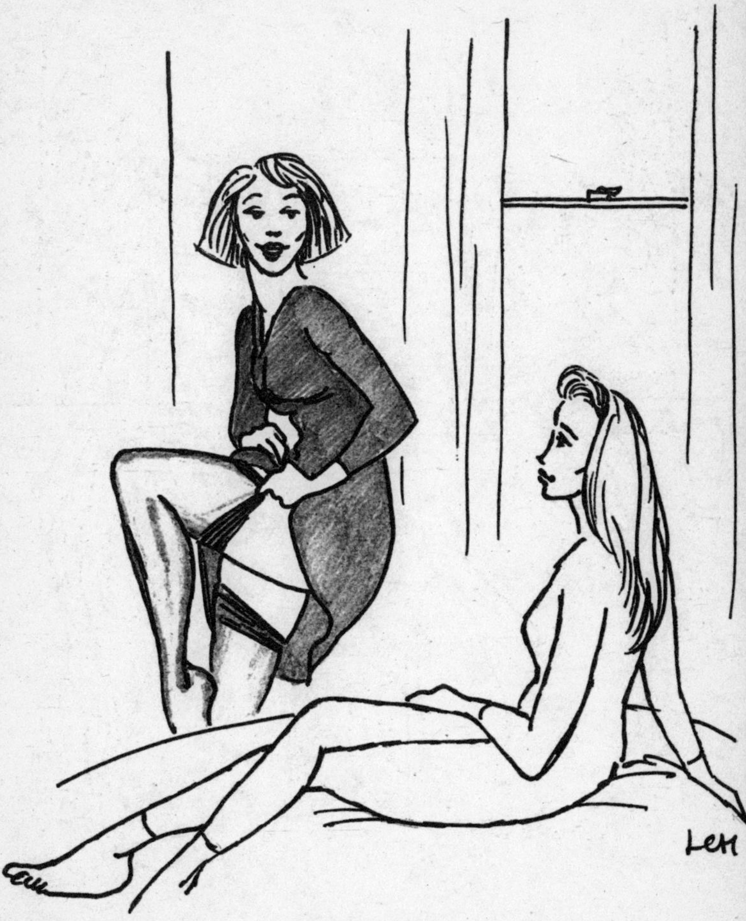

'It's not just that they're cool when it's hot, they make men so hot they're cool . . .'

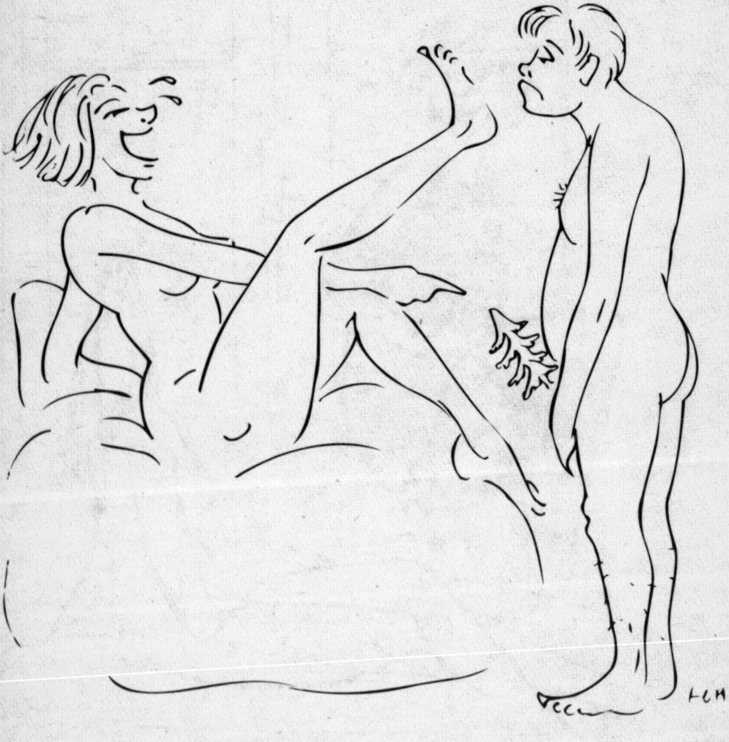
LCH

'Your condom needs pruning!'

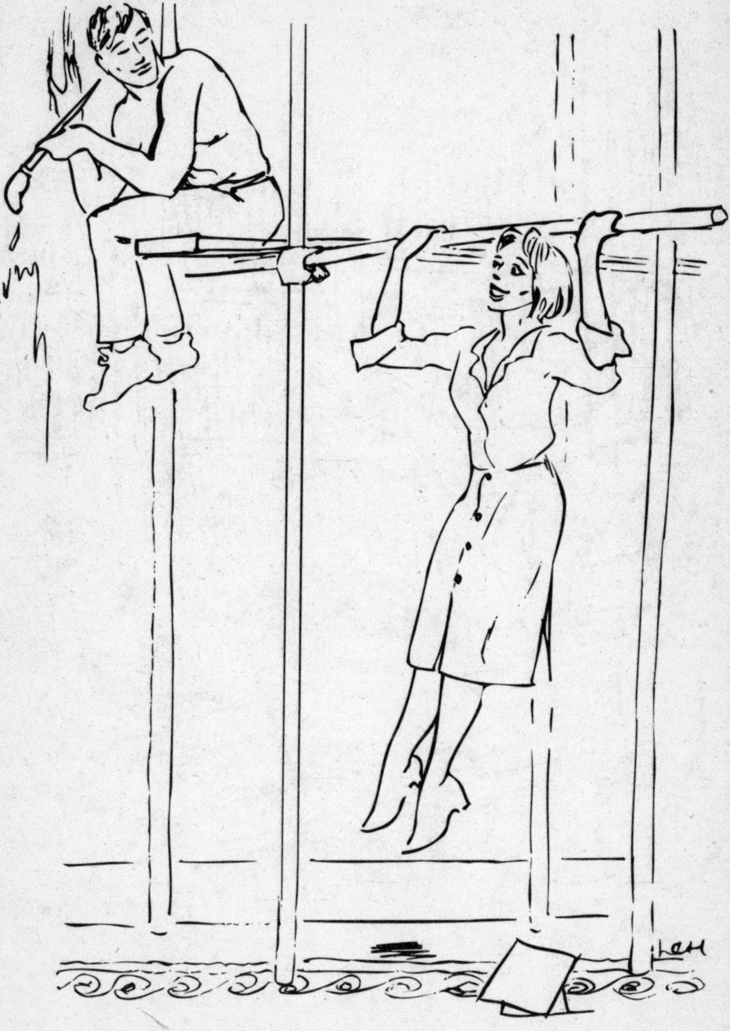

'Hi. Don't mind me hanging about, do you?'

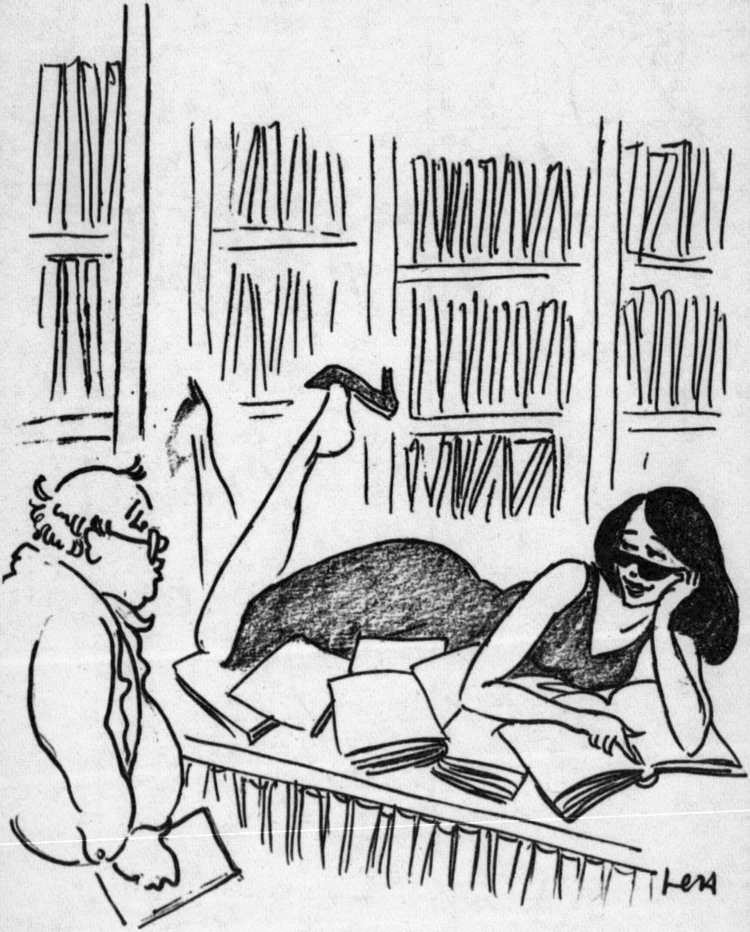

'Hi. This is the erotic section . . .'

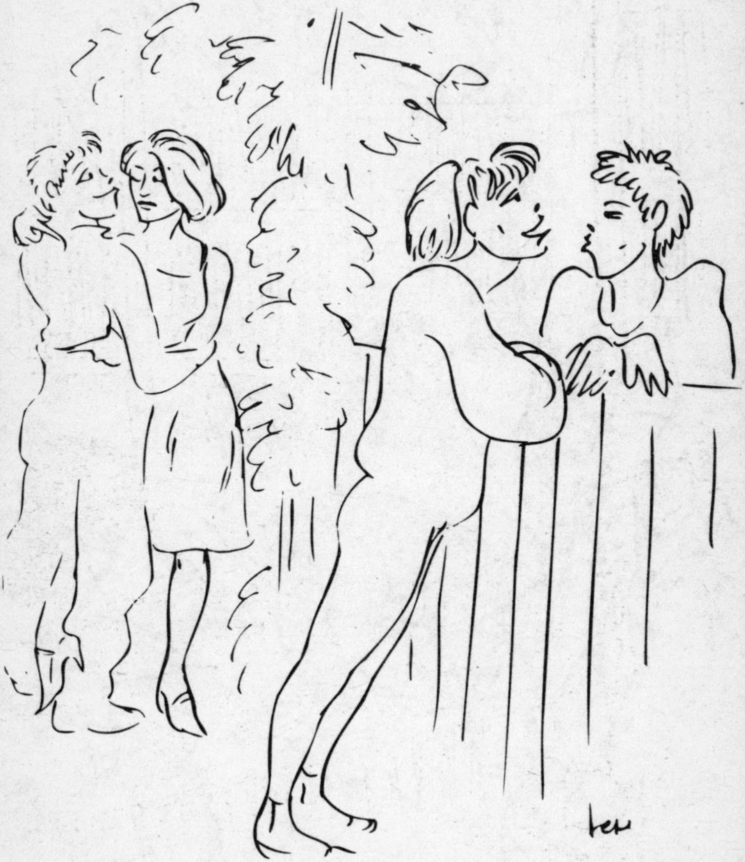

'Oh, he loves it when my mother comes.'

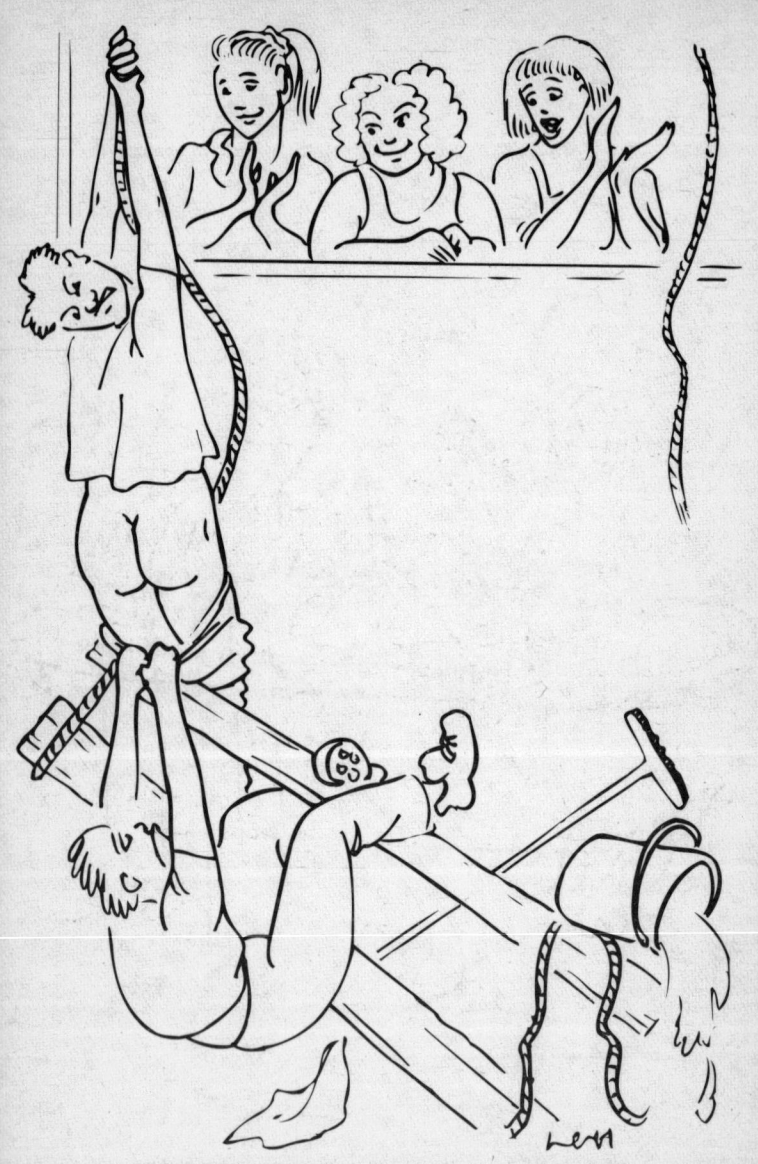

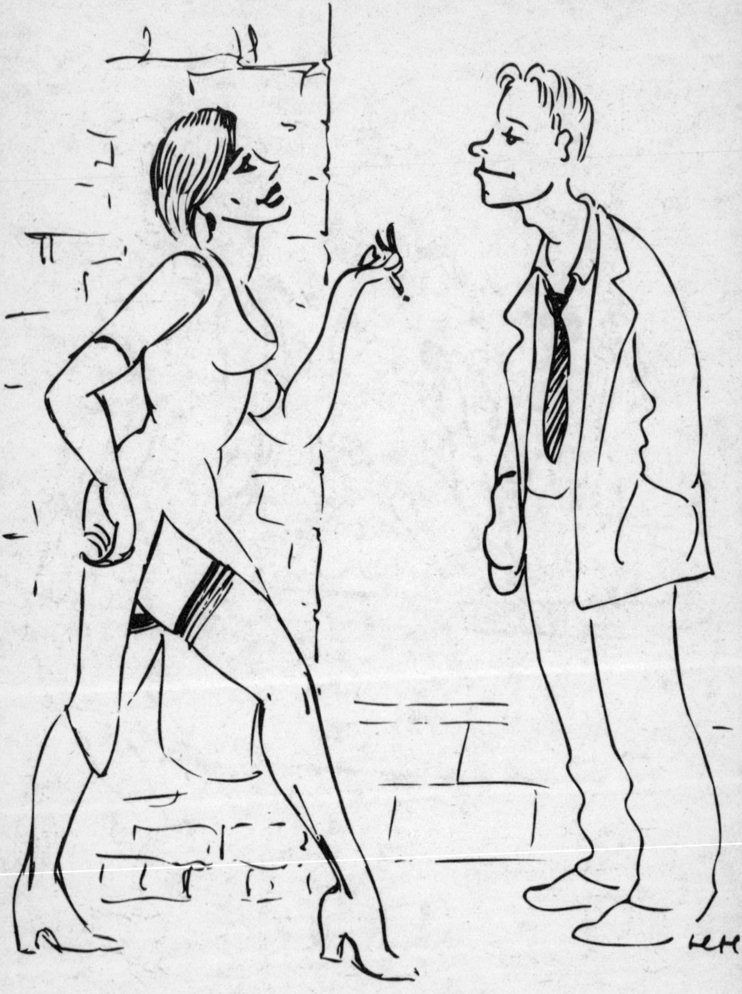
HH

'Hi, there. I'm waiting for a friend . . .
you look friendly.'

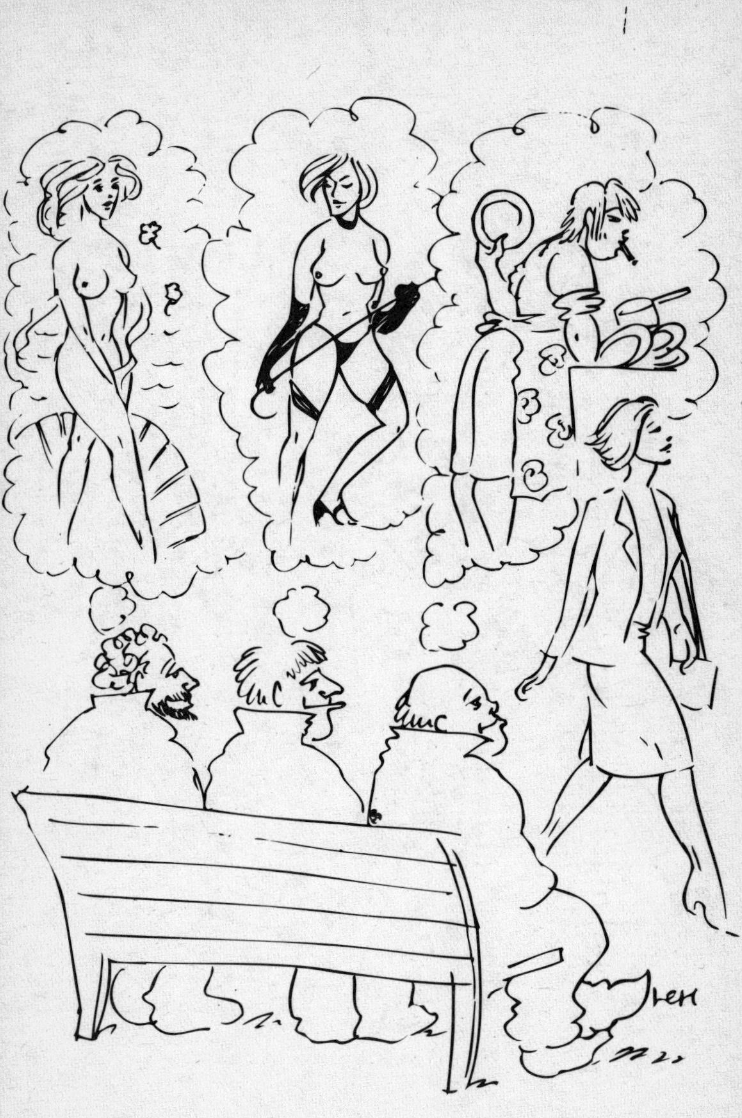

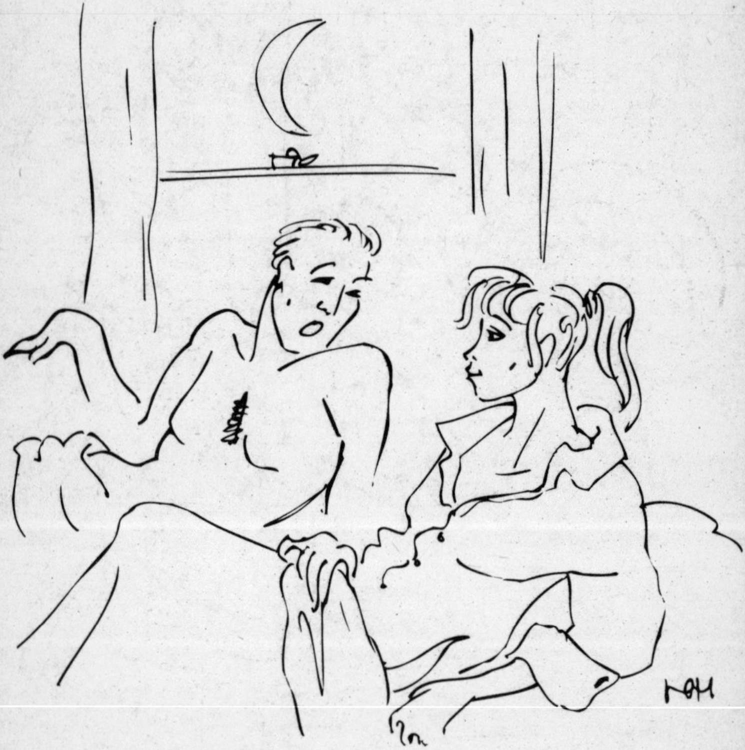

'The *difference* is, sweetheart, too many *beers,* and I throw up.'

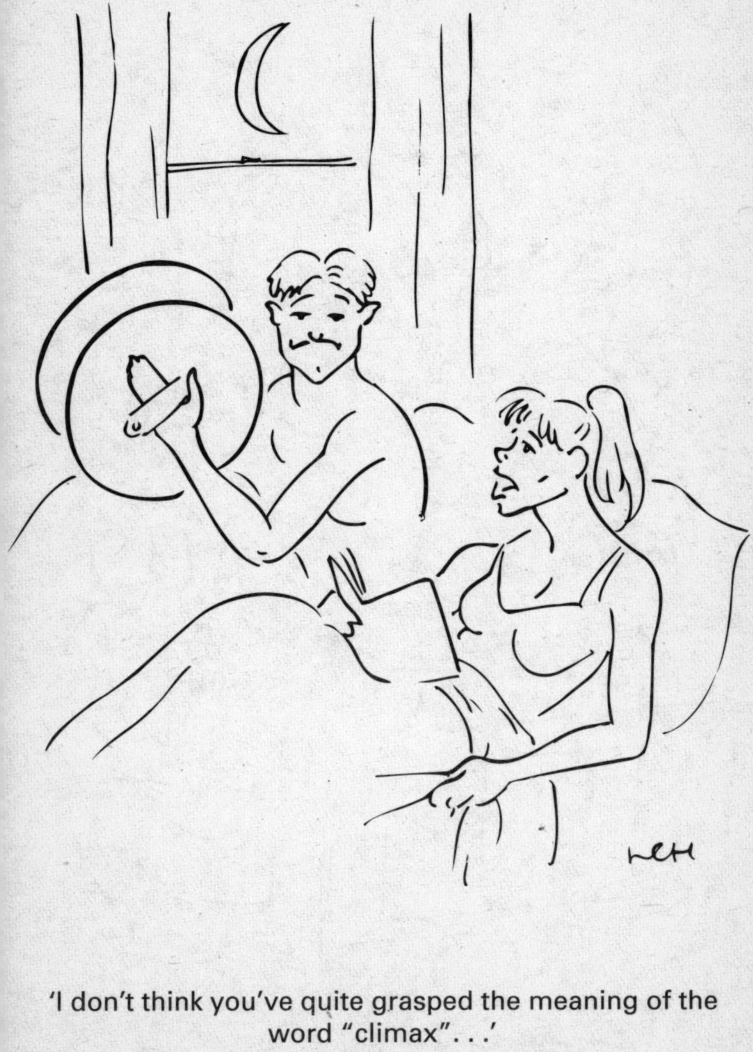

'I don't think you've quite grasped the meaning of the word "climax". . .'

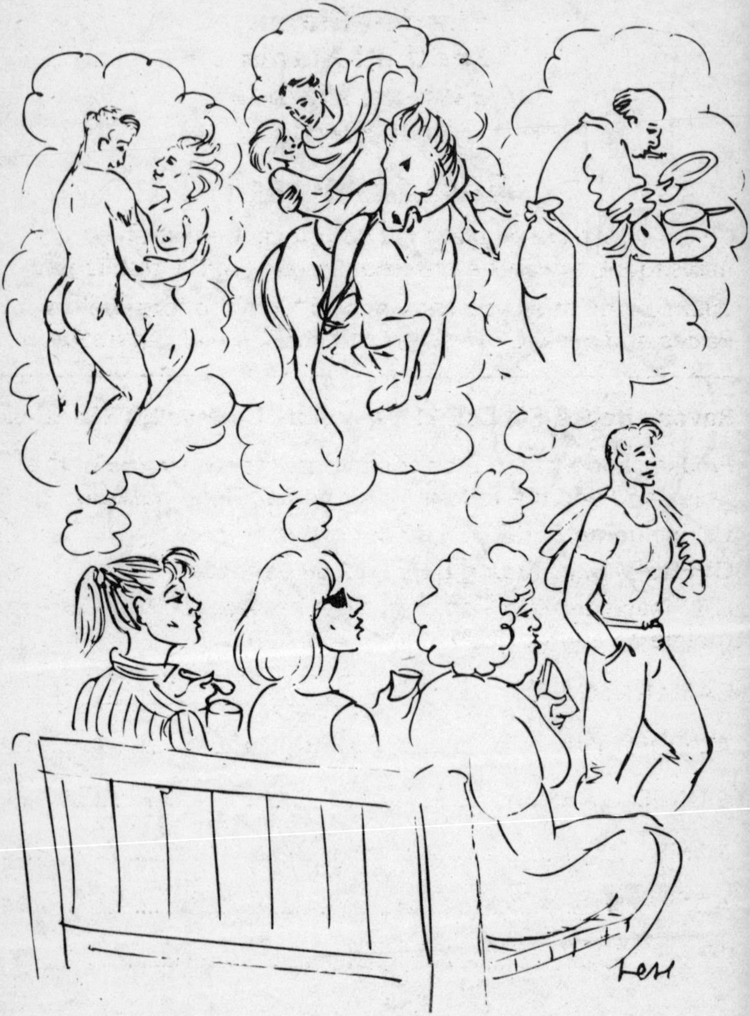

OTHER TITLES AVAILABLE IN THIS SERIES

Motor Mania
Garden Mania
Football Mania
Fishing Mania
Golf Mania

Price £2.50 each

These books are available at your local bookshop or newsagent, or can be ordered direct from the publisher.

Just tick the titles you require and fill in the form below. Prices and availability subject to change without notice.

Ravette Books, PO Box 11, Falmouth, Cornwall, TR10 9EN.

Please send a cheque or postal order for the value of the book, and add the following for postage and packing:

UK including BFPO – £1.00 per order.

OVERSEAS, including EIRE – £2.50 per order.

OR Please debit this amount from my Access/Visa Card (delete as appropriate).

CARD NUMBER ☐☐☐☐☐☐☐☐☐☐☐☐☐☐☐☐☐

AMOUNT £............................ EXPIRY DATE ....

SIGNED ....

NAME ....

ADDRESS ....

....

....

....